MW01519131

SUFISM IN EUROPE
AND NORTH AMERICA

Today there is a substantial and rapidly growing Muslim population in Europe and North America. Here, as elsewhere, many of the Muslims are Sufis. This book focuses mainly on issues of inculturation or contextualisation of Sufism in the West. It shows that, while more traditional forms of Sufism exist too, many radical changes have taken place in this part of the world. For instance, there are in some groups female sheikhs and a far-reaching pluralistic attitude to other religions. Hence, Sufism is sometimes seen as something that transcends the boundaries of Islam.

David Westerlund is Professor of Religious Studies at Södertörn University College in Stockholm and teaches also at the Universities of Uppsala and Gävle. His main interests are Islam in Africa and Europe, African indigenous religions and Christian–Muslim relations. He is currently the director of a multi-disciplinary project entitled 'Conflict or Peaceful Co-Existence? Contemporary Christian–Muslim Relations'.

SUFISM IN EUROPE AND NORTH AMERICA

Edited by
David Westerlund

RoutledgeCurzon
Taylor & Francis Group

LONDON AND NEW YORK

First published 2004
by RoutledgeCurzon
11 New Fetter Lane, London EC4P 4EE

Simultaneously published in the USA and Canada
by RoutledgeCurzon
29 West 35th Street, New York, NY 10001

RoutledgeCurzon is an imprint of the Taylor & Francis Group

© 2004 Editorial matter and selection, David Westerlund;
individual chapters, the contributors

Typeset in Sabon by
BOOK NOW Ltd
Printed and bound in Great Britain by
TJ International Ltd, Padstow, Cornwall

British Library Cataloguing in Publication Data
A catalogue record for this book is available from the British Library

Library of Congress Cataloging in Publication Data
A catalog record for this book has been requested

ISBN 0–415–32591–9

CONTENTS

CONTENTS

PREFACE

Due to the increased political significance of Islam, there has recently been a growing research interest in this world religion, focusing especially on Islamism. Likewise, it is above all the Islamist movements and organisations that have attracted media attention. By contrast, the fact that important changes have recently also taken place within Sufism, which is a most important movement within – as well as partly outside – Islam, has often been overlooked. Among the Western public at large, Sufism is largely associated with medieval thinkers like Ibn Arabi and Jalal al-Din Rumi, i.e. the Sufism of great philosophers and poets. Many of the intellectual Western converts to Islam have been attracted by this type of religion, and there are many books in Western languages, written by academic 'outsiders' as well as by Sufi 'insiders', on classical Sufism of this kind. Mainly due to research carried out by social scientists, there are now also a considerable number of works that focus on political and socio-economic aspects of Sufism in predominantly Muslim parts of the world.

Hitherto, however, the presence of Sufism in the West has not been the object of much research. The aim of this book, which focuses primarily on modern changes associated with the inculturation or contextualisation of Sufism in Europe and North America, is to contribute to remedying this deficiency. The contributions are written in an essayistic style, and the volume is intended not only for scholars and students but for a wide circle of readers. Some of the essays here have previously been published in Swedish in a book entitled *Levande sufism* (2001). These contributions have been revised and translated into English by the authors themselves. The present volume has been produced partly within the context of a research project called 'Conflict or Peaceful Co-Existence? Contemporary Christian–Muslim Relations'; and the relationship of Sufism to the Christian and secular environment in the West is one of the book's central themes. For valuable suggestions during the process of editing this book, I express my gratitude to Ingvar Svanberg, one of my colleagues on this project.

David Westerlund
Stockholm
October 2003

CONTRIBUTORS

Ravil Bukharaev is a writer and journalist with the BBC World Service. He has for a number of years been engaged in research on Islam, focusing on historical as well as contemporary Muslim societies in Russia. His most recent books in this field are *Islam in Russia: Four Models* (2000), *Model of Tatarstan* (1999) and *Historical Anthology of Kazan Tatar Verse* (2000), which he co-edited with D. J. Matthews.

Ian K. B. Draper is a Research Fellow at the Department of Theology, University of Birmingham, where he received his Ph.D. in Islamic Studies after presenting a thesis entitled 'Towards a Postmodern Sufism: Eclecticism, Appropriation and Adaptation in a Qadiriyya and Naqshbandiyya Tariqa in the UK' (2002), at which time he was known as Mustafa Draper. He was the main UK and Internet fieldworker for a major research project on transnational Sufism, sponsored by the British Economic and Social Research Council, and has previously completed ethnographic research on the Naqshbandiyya Ghamkol Sharif in Britain.

Olav Hammer is Assistant Professor at the Department of Religious Studies, Amsterdam University. His interests are centred on various aspects of religious innovation in the contemporary West, such as the adaptation of religious discourse to a post-Enlightenment context and the effects of globalisation. Among other things, he has published the book *Claiming Knowledge: Strategies of Epistemology from Theosophy to the New Age* (2001).

Marcia Hermansen received her Ph.D. from the University of Chicago, where she was a student of Fazlur Rahman. She is now Professor of Theology at Loyola University, Chicago, where she teaches courses on Islamic studies and world religions. Her recent publications include the monograph *The Conclusive Argument for God* (1996), which is a study and translation (from Arabic) of Shah Wali Allah's *Hujjat Allah al-Baligha*, and numerous articles in the fields of Islamic thought, Sufism, Islam and Muslims in South Asia, Muslims in America and women in Islam.

Thomas McElwain earned a Ph.D. in Comparative Religion at the University of Stockholm with a thesis on Native American narrative, and became an Associate Professor there in 1981, last serving as Director of Interfaith Dialogue at the Islamic Centre of England in London (2001–2). Among other things, he has done field research on Sufism in Turkey. In addition to numerous scholarly publications, which include the long essay 'Ritual Change in a Turkish Alevi Village', in *The Problem of Ritual* (ed. Tore Ahlbäck, 1993), he has written many apologetical works on Islam and the Dawoodi-Bektashi order, in which he is active.

Garbi Schmidt is Research Fellow and Director of the ethnic minority programme at the Danish National Institute of Social Research in Copenhagen. She specialises in Muslim minorities in the United States and Scandinavia. Her recent writings include *Islam in Urban America* (2004) and 'Dialectics of Authenticity: Examples of Ethnification of Islam among Young Muslims in the United States and Denmark', in *The Muslim World* (spring issue 2002).

Ingvar Svanberg is an ethnologist and Senior Research Fellow at the Department of East European Studies, Uppsala University. His research interests include Central Asia, Islam in Europe, minority issues and ethnobiology. He has written numerous books and articles on a wide range of topics, including *China's Last Nomads* (1998) and *Contemporary Kazaks* (1999), and co-edited, with David Westerlund, *Islam Outside the Arab World* (1999).

David Westerlund is Professor of Religious Studies at the new Södertörn University College in Stockholm and teaches the

History of Religions at the Faculty of Theology, Uppsala University. He is engaged in research on Islam in Africa and Europe, Christian–Muslim relations and African indigenous religions. His recent publications include the collective volumes *Questioning the Secular State: The Worldwide Resurgence of Religion in Politics* (1996) and *African Islam and Islam in Africa: Encounters between Sufis and Islamists* (1997), which he co-edited with Eva Evers Rosander.

1

INTRODUCTION

Inculturating and transcending Islam

David Westerlund

The term Sufism probably derives from the Arabic word for wool, *suf*. Cloaks made of wool were used by early Sufis as a symbol of poverty and privation. Occasionally it may still happen that a cloak is given to someone who is being initiated into a Sufi order, *tariqa* (pl. *turuq*). The word Sufism has also been associated with *safa*, which means purity. Some people, who have stressed the wisdom dimension of Sufism, have wanted to derive Sufism from the Greek term for wisdom (*sophos*, *sophia*). Although this suggested origin is unlikely, this way of reasoning is an intimation of the connections between Sufism and certain Greek conceptions.

Background

No religious movement arises from a vacuum. It is affected by, as well as influences, the context in which it develops. The wool cloak is one of many examples of points of contact between early Sufism and Christianity, particularly the Syrian–Nestorian tradition. Early Sufi Muslims were influenced by, among other things, Christian ways of praying, asceticism and certain monastic ideals. For many of them, Jesus served as an ascetic model, although celibacy did not become a Sufi ideal. The early Sufis were individualists who lacked a fixed organisation. By degrees, however, a rudimentary form of organisation evolved. Group meetings were centred around a prayer called *dhikr* (remembrance), which sometimes developed into a form of religious concert (*sama*). In addition to Christian influences, early Sufi Muslims were inspired by, among other things, Neoplatonic and Gnostic ideas. When Sufism eventually spread further and further into different parts of the world, it developed, in interplay with many different religious traditions, into an exceedingly varied phenomenon.

While some Sufi leaders were religious scholars, *ulama*, who were also representatives of official or 'orthodox' Islam, sanctioned by the powers that be, others were more critical of political establishments. The luxurious life of the Ummayad caliph in Damascus and his associates clashed with Sufi ideals of poverty and altruistic serving. As time went on, the tensions and conflicts between Sufis and representatives of establishment Islam grew and reached a peak in the tenth and eleventh centuries. One important reason for this culmination was the release of Sufism from official control. Officially, Sufis were criticised for doctrinal deviations and shortcomings in terms of ritual observations. In 922, the Sufi Husayn Ibn Mansur al-Hallaj was executed, accused of having claimed to be divine. As a result of, among other things, this extreme event, some Sufis began to come nearer officially sanctioned forms of Islam. Abu Hamid al-Ghazali (d. 1111) is often given the credit for an important rapprochement and reconciliation between Sufis and 'orthodox' Muslims. He opposed what he saw as certain extremes among both Sufis and *ulama*. First and foremost, however, he was an intellectually outstanding representative of the Abbasid establishment, if influenced by a 'sober' and ethically oriented type of Sufism.

From the eleventh and twelfth centuries, the activities that were centred around a meeting-place, *zawiya*, and its leading Sufi sheikh or pir, developed into a more firmly organised institution. The orders that were established eventually became of great importance in the rapidly growing Muslim areas. In the orders, which were usually named after the founding sheikhs, the disciples were initiated into different levels of spiritual maturity. Leaders appointed successors who could refer to a chain, *silsila*, of predecessors. Through this genealogy and the special power or blessing called *baraka*, the sheikhs had a preferential right of interpretation and were associated with healing and other wonders. Veneration of deceased sheikhs or saints frequently became important in popular forms of Sufism, and places where they were buried became pilgrimage sites.

Through its firm organisation and accelerated expansion, Sufism became represented in all social layers of society, and its social, economic and political roles became increasingly important. Some Sufi sheikhs supported political leaders and contributed to the legitimation of their exercise of power, while others could lead resistance and revolts against such leaders. Due to their widely spread networks, particularly the main orders – in the same way as the Roman Catholic Church – could sometimes wield strong resistance against territorial states. Orders and *zawiyas* in urban centres usually had a closer relation to *ulama* than had Sufi Muslims who lived in the countryside, where the distance to establishment Islam and its representatives tended to be greater.

Today there are about two hundred 'mother orders', but since smaller and bigger branches have continuously grown from the trunks, the total number of *tariqa* organisations is much bigger than that. Some ten stand out as particularly important and widespread. Most of these, as well as some of their branches, are mentioned or treated in more detail in different places in this book. The orders differ from each other because of, among other things, their various forms of piety, doctrinal systems and practices associated, especially, with their founders. Throughout history, a number of reforms have occurred too. A strikingly significant part of the Islamic 'mission', or *dawa*, oriented towards non-Muslims, has been carried out by Sufi Muslims, who have usually shown a marked flexibility in their relationship to other religions and cultures.

After a certain stagnancy from the late medieval ages, Sufism in some areas began expanding rapidly again during the nineteenth and twentieth centuries. This modern spread occurred above all in Africa south of the Sahara, where it, paradoxically, coincided with the expansion of European colonialism but also continued after that. The missionary endeavours of Sufis, as well as of other Muslims, were facilitated by, among other things, new and improved means of communication and, in some regions like northern Nigeria and German East Africa, colonial administration policies. In some areas, however, Sufi orders spearheaded resistance against colonial rule. The inclusivity that largely characterised both expanding Sufi orders and African indigenous religions formed a good breeding ground for the formation of new syntheses with Muslim designations. Sufi mission attitudes often contrasted sharply with the strong early Christian missionary condemnations of African 'paganism'. During the twentieth century, the spread of Sufism in the West became increasingly important too. As will be shown in some of the essays in this book, this expansion occurred both through active missionary work and, above all, because of migration from predominantly Muslim parts of the world to the West.

The contributions to this book

It is not easy to present adequately such a multifarious and wide-spread entity as Sufism in Europe and North America. However, by focusing on different regions, orders and themes, the essays in this book depict a great deal of the far-reaching variety of Sufi ideas and practices. Much emphasis is put on studies of the effects of the contextualisation or integration of Sufism in the West – with a term borrowed from Christian mission studies, we may also speak about its inculturation. While the first three contributions are broader overviews of various regions, the others provide more specialised and detailed accounts. In this section of the introduction the different essays will be presented briefly, after which follows another section on some particularly important thematic issues.

In the first contribution, David Westerlund starts off with a discussion of various types of Islam in Europe, thus placing Sufism within a wider Islamic context. With references mainly to Western Europe, he then exemplifies the presence of important classical orders such as Naqshbandiyya and Nimatullahiyya, both with a primarily Asian origin, as well as Qadiriyya and Tijaniyya, which have entered Europe largely with immigrants from Africa. Wester-lund also presents some of the new types of Sufism, and in the final part of his essay he focuses on Sufi theologies of religion. Here he exemplifies, among other things, how in some forms of what he calls 'Euro-Sufism' there is a tendency to transcend Islam in favour of a more generally religious position. Among Sufi perennialists like René Guénon and Frithjof Schuon, for instance, there is an idea that the esoteric kernel of the ageless wisdom (*philosophia perennis*) or religion (*religio perennis*), is found not only in Islam but also in other religions like Christianity and Hinduism. Westerlund emphasises that leaders of traditional orders, such as the Nimatullahi grand sheikh Jawad Nurbakhsh, who are active in the West, also tend to show great openness vis-à-vis other religions like Christianity. Moreover, it is stressed that in the 'strong societies' of Europe, Sufism basically lacks some of the social and economic functions it has in many predominantly Muslim countries and that Sufi women often have more prominent roles in Europe than in such countries.

As in Europe, female leadership and participation in Sufi contexts is a striking feature in North America too. The role of women is one of the aspects highlighted in the contribution by Marcia Hermansen, who remarks that Sufism has quickly adopted to the American context. Features such as individualism, voluntarism and experiential modes of spirituality, as well as the strong emphasis on the separation of religion and state, have tended to favour the spread of Sufism. Hermansen stresses the diversity of Sufism in the United States and points out that while Caucasians and African Americans are attracted primarily by perennial and hybrid forms of an intellectual and elitist kind, more popular varieties of Sufi Islam are found mainly among immigrants. However, the latter type of Sufism is less frequent here than in Europe, where immigrant Muslims in general are less highly educated. The strong African American involvement in Sufi circles is one of the factors that have contributed to a 'domestication' of Sufism in North America. Among other things, Hermansen emphasises that, to some extent, Sufism is part of a 'psychologisation' of religion, and many sheikhs add psychology and psychotherapy to their spiritual training. In the promotion and advertising of their message and activities, Sufi groups frequently use media, including the Internet.

Although Islam in most parts of Europe is a young religion, there are a few areas where it has a long history. In addition to southern Europe, especially the Iberian peninsula, and the Balkans, Russia belongs to these regions. Thus, the contribution by Ravil Bukharaev provides a quite detailed account of the historical development of Sufism in this huge country of Eastern Europe from its beginnings in the ninth century, with special reference to the Volga–Urals area. In a way, Sufism could benefit from the medieval Mongol demolition of 'orthodox' Muslim institutions and hierarchies. However, particularly after the time of Ivan the Terrible in the sixteenth century, Sufism – like other forms of Islam – became a sharply persecuted faith. To some degree the suppressed minority situation contributed to softening intra-Islamic tensions between Sufis and non-Sufi Muslims. When reformist movements, particularly Jadidism, started developing in the nineteenth century, there were several Sufis who played leading roles. In the late twentieth century, however, orders like the Naqshbandiyya and Qadiriyya were put under strong pressure from the growth of anti-Sufi Islamist groups, especially in violence-ridden areas like Chechnya and Daghestan. This added substantially to the problems that had already been caused by anti-religious policies during the period of Soviet rule. According to Bukharaev, Sufism in Russia is today in a weak position, although new eclectic and ecumenically oriented groups have managed to attract some followers in this part of Europe too.

An eclectic Sufi order with a long history in Eastern Europe, particularly in the Ottoman empire, is the Bektashiyya. In the present, post-Communist era there are signs of revival in several parts of the Balkans. In his essay on Bektashi dervishes, Thomas McElwain also traces their spread further west in Europe and North America. He stresses, among other things, the traditionally unusual integration of men and women in ritual and other contexts. For instance, in ritual dances both sexes may take part. The relatively free relationships between men and women, as well as several other characteristics of the Bektashi order, such as shamanistic and Christian influences, have contributed to occasioning strong criticism from 'orthodox' Muslims. The fact that Sufism has often been much influenced by different religions has already been touched upon. However, in the Bektashi order the amalgamation of beliefs and practices with different origins is particularly conspicuous. In addition to more obvious sources of inspiration, McElwain discusses some examples of possible Jewish influence too. The Sufi master who gave the order its name, Hajji Bektash, held that different people have various needs, which legitimates a far-reaching doctrinal tolerance. Arguably, this openness and flexibility has facilitated the spread of the Bektashiyya in the West.

Following McElwain's account of this eclectic order of dervishes, there are two thematic contributions. In an essay on a branch of the Naqshbandi order, Garbi Schmidt analyses the role of the Internet. With home pages of the Naqshbandi-Haqqaniyya, whose grand sheikh is Muhammad Nazim al-Haqqani from Cyprus, as her main source, she asks whether the 'traditionalised charisma' that characterises Sufi sheikhs can work via this medium, and her answer is affirmative. Schmidt's account focuses on Nazim's leading representative in the United States, Sheikh Hisham Muhammad Kabbani. She concludes that the home pages are intended for a global circle of readers – their texts are rendered in several languages – and that the central position of the leading sheikhs is emphasised. In the Internet material the common tension between Sufis and Islamists is a recurring feature. Hisham Kabbani has argued strongly against Islamistically inspired Muslims who, in turn, have polemicised sharply against him and his Sufi message. In this debate, he stresses, among other things, that those who interpret Islam must have a legitimate authority to do so.

A modern Sufi movement where women, even in leadership positions, have achieved great significance is one that was initiated by the Indian Sheikh Hazrat Inayat Khan, who as early as in 1910 started his work of spreading a Sufi message in the West. In the essay by Olav Hammer on 'Sufism for Westerners', he discusses in detail the universalism represented by, among others, Khan as well as Frithjof Schuon and Idries Shah. In addition, Hammer compares this to the more thoroughly Islam-based Sufism of Fadhlalla Haeri, another sheikh with the Western world as his 'mission field', highlighting some of its characteristics. With regard to the universalistically oriented forms of Sufism, Hammer stresses, in addition to new gender roles and individualism, the interest in psychology and the focus on experiences rather than correct praxis. He argues that at a time and in a context where New Age is an important phenomenon, it is likely that this type of Sufism has better opportunities of growth than the more Islam-oriented alternatives.

In a local study of Sufism in the town of Glastonbury in southwest England, Ian K. B. Draper focuses, in particular, on the Naqshbandi-Haqqaniyya. Of particular significance in this town is the Tor, a steep natural hill that has been a centre of religious associations for centuries past, especially pre-Christian and modern pagan ones. Adherents of Haqqaniyya and other orders in Glastonbury deemphasise the Islamic connections of Sufism and have a universalistic approach. While some Sufis here relate to pre-Christian Celtic as well as neo-shamanic ideas, the Haqqani followers, whose grand sheikh Nazim visited this town in 1999, orient themselves more towards Christianity. One feature of Sufism here, as in many other places, is the presence of both sexes in meetings. With his local perspective from a context influenced to a considerable degree by New Age ideas, Draper thus exemplifies some of the general remarks made by Hammer and others about universalistically oriented Sufis.

Although research on Sufism in the West is still largely in its infancy, there are now a number of publications available, and the book ends with a select bibliography of such works. This has been compiled by Ingvar Svanberg. In addition to the bibliographic information about important works on Sufism in the West, there are also some important examples of more general works on Sufism.

Some thematic issues

Contrary to some notions about contemporary Sufism, the contributions to this book show that it has not become set in a fixed mould but is a most dynamic movement. In several respects it thus undergoes changes. However, there are also examples of the conservative role of Sufism, although this side is less accentuated in this book. In predominantly Muslim countries in the so-called third world, Sufi orders are often strong in countryside areas, while Islamists tend to be well represented in urban settings, which are more strongly affected by the influences of modernity. Islamists frequently criticise Sufis because the type of Islam they represent is mixed with beliefs and practices of non-Islamic origin. The former, thus, argue that the Islam of the latter must be 'purified' from *bida* (innovation), i.e. such things that are held to contradict the Quran and the customs of the prophet Muhammad (*sunna*), which form the main basis of Islamic law (*sharia*).

Islamists usually argue that the precondition for a morally just situation is that God and His law are allowed to govern society as well as individuals. This focus on Islam as law and as a basis of society is another reason for the tensions between Islamists and Sufis, even though there are also many Sufis who stress the importance of the exoteric dimensions of Islam. The brief historical background above shows that Islamists are certainly not the first ones to criticise Sufis for neglecting or not paying enough attention to the 'outer' side of Islam. Unlike Sufi sheikhs and *ulama*, who normally have a more traditional Islamic training, leaders of Islamist movements are often educated in modern schools of technology and the sciences rather than in theology or Islamic law. Among others, Hassan al-Turabi, the Sudanese leader of the Muslim Brotherhood – one of the internationally most important Islamist organisations – has argued that the term *ulama* should be widened to include people with a higher education other than the traditionally religious one. Sufi sheikhs, on the other hand, may claim that they have a preferential right of interpretation because of their religious schooling and particular blessing (*baraka*) as well as the chain (*silsila*) that connects them to previous masters and spiritually legitimates their authority to interpret Islam. According to Sufi – as well as Shia – ideas, there is an esoteric dimension of the Quran which only those leaders who are spiritually legitimated can interpret, and Sufi sheikhs may have a priest-like function as intermediaries between God and humans. This function is criticised by Islamists, who oppose the preferential right of interpretation claimed by sheikhs and other traditional authorities and stress the idea that all humans are directly accountable to God.

As exemplified in some of the essays in this book, the issue of authority to interpret sacred texts and lead Muslims becomes central. Is this authority based on a certain position, legitimated by *baraka*, *silsila* and esotericism, or can in principle anyone with proper knowledge be a leader? In criticism of Islamists as 'lay persons', grand sheikhs like Nazim al-Haqqani and Hisham Kabbani can assert their authority and preferential right of interpretation by referring to traditional schooling as well as to specific Sufi arguments as mentioned above. It should be pointed out, however, that the borderline between Sufism and Islamism is not always sharp. Perhaps the clearest example in the West of blurring this divide is the Murabitun, founded by the British actor Ian Dallas, whose Muslim name is Abd al-Qadir. This sheikh now emphasises strongly that Sufism must not be separated from the political, socio-economic and legal aspects of Islam.

In recent years, the concept of globalisation has been widely used. Among other things, it indicates that the world has become 'smaller' or more 'dense' in the sense that different people and outlooks on life are now in closer contact with each other. One important aspect of globalisation is the rapid spread of the English language as a means of communication across national and continental boundaries. No language has previously had such a strong global position as English has today. Through its orders, Sufism retains its organisational strength and widens its already widely spread international ramifications. English now clearly complements and is gradually replacing Arabic as the most important means of communication across language barriers. More and more Sufi literature is published in English, and in the use of new media, particularly the Internet, this language has a powerful position too. Use of the Internet has become important, especially for small Sufi groups – as well as for other small religious organisations – because it gives an opportunity to reach out with the message at a very low cost. In Europe and North America, where great numbers of people use the Internet, it is of particular significance. However, in those parts of the world where only small minorities of people have access to the Internet, other media like cassettes and radio programmes may be more important.

The language change is partly connected to substantial religious and social innovations, which are an important and exciting field of research. One of the significant changes that are partly associated with the spread of Sufism in the West, and Western influence in predominantly Muslim countries, concerns the relationship between the sexes. Changes in terms of gender roles can be seen especially in Sufi groups who above all focus on establishing themselves in the West. There are examples of such changes in several of the contributions to this book. Even though female sheikhs and *zawiyas* are not entirely new phenomena, the mixing of the sexes that increasingly occurs in Western Sufi services and meetings is essentially an innovation.

The intensive and liberal theological rethinking that is taking place among many Sufis and other Muslims who are directly confronted with Western conditions may in the long run have repercussions on predominantly Muslim parts of the world too. One of the fields that is treated in several of the essays is the religio-theological, i.e. the issue of how Sufis should relate to people who belong to other religions, especially Christianity. The tendency towards a pluralist theology of religion that traditionally charac-terises Islam, and Sufism in particular, is often strengthened by the encounter with the West. This tendency can be seen, for instance, in the preaching of sheikh Nazim, who is in close touch with collaborators and disciples in the West. Above all, it can be noticed among some Sufi leaders who live and work in Europe or North America. In their thinking, Sufism transcends the boundaries between many or all religions to the point where it is argued that a person can be a Sufi without having an Islamic identity. It seems reasonable to assume that for those who adhere to a strictly univer-salist position, missionary activities would not be very important. In practice this often seems to be the case too – perennialists, for instance, are seldom characterised by a fervent missionary interest. Paradoxically, however, there are some universalistically oriented Sufis with such an interest. One example is Hazrat Inayat Khan, whose vision was that if human beings were convinced by his universal message of love, harmony and beauty, then the East and the West could be united.

The idea of Sufism as a bridge between 'East and West' is also found in the title of McElwain's essay in this book; and in his contribution, Westerlund refers, among other things, to a statement by the British perennialist Martin Lings, who argues that Sufism can serve as such a bridge because it stresses the connections between Islam and other religions. Another argument was accentuated by the late Swedish anthropologist Tomas Gerholm, who, in a collected volume edited by Akbar S. Ahmed and Hastings Donnan, *Islam, Globalization and Postmodernity* (1994), stated that 'Sufism *can* be a compromise between East and West: it is private enough to fit into the Western social order and it is public enough to remain an echo of the total Islamic order' (p. 207). These are interesting ideas. Yet it should be restated that Sufism is a most varied phenomenon and that, consequently, some forms of Sufism may work better than others as bridges between various parts of the world.

In his book *Le soufisme* (1984), published in the well-known French series 'Que sais-je?', Jean Chevalier concludes that the genuine Sufism is the one that is turned inwards. Now it is not the duty of scholars to decide which kind of Sufism is authentic or not. The present volume provides examples of different kinds of Sufism. Mysticism, or the inner side, is certainly a central part of Sufism. Poetry, music and art are unquestionably important aspects too, even though this book does not focus on those. However, it is good that the numerous studies of mystical and, in the more narrow sense, cultural dimensions of Sufism have recently been supplemented by an increasing number of works that focus on, among other things, political and socio-economic issues. This change is partly caused by the fact that an increasing number of social scientists and social-science-influenced scholars of religion have become interested in Sufism and other forms of Islam or religion.

Perhaps there is a risk that, in the long run, there will be a new one-sidedness, so that the religious and cultural aspects of Sufism become marginalised in the research. The studies of, for instance, the Muridiyya, which is a West African offshoot of the Qadiriyya, may exemplify this risk of a new bias. Thus there are now many fine works on the political, social and economic significance of the Muridiyya but few very well-informed accounts of its religious and cultural dimensions. Portraits of, for example, this order – be they painted by scholars or others – are always slanted and incomplete. In order to produce knowledge that is as balanced and ample as possible, it is thus important that different scholars with various angles of approach, i.e. different concepts of religion, interests and disciplinary specialisation, contribute to the study of Sufism. It goes without saying that the collected and, over time, changing picture will also be influenced by the factual development of Sufism. Hopefully, this volume will provide some important clues for a prognosis of what this development will look like. By focusing mainly on religious aspects of Sufism in the West, and especially on its partly new forms in this part of the world, the essays here will complement other studies that concentrate more on socio-economic and political dimensions.

2

THE CONTEXTUALISATION OF SUFISM IN EUROPE

David Westerlund

During certain periods of time the presence of Islam has been strongly felt in southern Europe. This applies in particular to the Iberian peninsula in the Middle Ages and the Balkans under Ottoman rule. Even now, in the early 2000s, there are high numbers of Muslims in countries of south-eastern Europe, especially in Albania and Bosnia. In some southern parts of Russia, Islam has a long and important history too. During recent decades, the number of Muslims in other parts of Europe has increased rapidly, mainly because of labour immigration and the arrival of refugees from predominantly Muslim parts of the world. Countries with a colonial past, particularly France and Great Britain, now have substantial Muslim minorities. While the majority of the British Muslims originally came from South Asia, most of France's Muslims have a North African, especially Algerian, origin. In Germany, the Muslims have a primarily Turkish background. However, since a large-scale immigration of Muslims to Central, Western and Northern Europe has now continued for more than half a century, the majority of Europe's Muslims were born here. Thus the influence of second- and third-generation Muslims in the shaping of Islam in this part of the world is now of vital significance.

It is only to a quite limited extent that the number of Muslims in Europe has increased because of conversions. Yet converts to Islam form a group of people who, partly because they have European languages as their mother tongue, know the cultural codes well and are often highly educated, and in many cases they can function as spokespersons for Muslims. In that way their influence can be much more important than their limited numbers may indicate. In several of the surprisingly few studies there are on Muslims in contemporary Europe, it has been concluded that Sufism is a branch of Islam that seems to be particularly attractive to Europeans. On the whole, Sufism has a very strong position in Europe, as in other parts of the world. Both in Eastern Europe and among Muslims who have immigrated from Asia and Africa, various Sufi orders and movements have a strong position. In order to place Sufism in a wider Islamic context an analytical pattern concerning contemporary currents among Muslims in Europe will first be outlined. Then an overview of various types of Sufism will be presented. Finally, the chapter will focus on Sufi theologies of religion, i.e. views on other religions, particularly Christianity. There, in particular, it will be shown how Sufism is becoming contextualised or inculturated in Europe.

Islam in European contexts

Characterising Muslims and people with some Muslim background, we may differentiate between four types. We can think of a line where the extremes are represented by, on the one side, secularised people with a Muslim background and, on the other side, Islamists. Between these extremes there are representatives of what might be called the Muslim mainstream and Euro-Islam.

Clearly, Muslims who have come to Europe have been exposed to a strong pressure of secularisation which has influenced many of them. As a result, some have become agnostics or atheists. Others have kept their religious beliefs, even if they have been weakened, but have stopped practising Islam, at least officially. There are also examples of the reverse, i.e. Muslims who are no longer believers but who still – largely for social reasons – to some degree continue practising, for instance on Muslim holidays. Moreover, it should be noticed that some Muslims who have emigrated to Europe were already secularised before arriving here. In particular, a considerable number of Iranians who have come to Europe fled from Iran because of their dissociation from Ayatullah Khomeini and the Islamic Republic. Even though the Muslims who no longer believe in

God and have stopped practising Islam are most likely a very small minority, it is probably a growing group.

Islamist movements and organisations, which during recent decades have fought for the strengthening of Islam in predominantly Muslim countries, are in various ways represented in Europe too. A particularly important group of associations are those that are affiliated to the Muslim Brotherhood, which is an internationally widely spread movement with its roots in an Egyptian organisation founded in the early 1920s by Hassan al-Banna. European Islamists now work in various organisations, which are more or less radical but usually belong to the moderate branch of the Islamist movement, in order to strengthen the Muslim adherence to Islam. They emphasise the significance of Islam as a comprehensive way of life or system of rules and often plead for a Muslim right to some amount of separate legislation, for instance concerning slaughtering. Clearly, it is particularly difficult to predict the future of Islamism in Europe. Presumably, however, it will largely depend on the global Islamist success or decline. Within Europe the socio-economic development and the reactions of the non-Muslim majorities will probably be of decisive importance for its development. An Islamist-influenced 'ghetto Islam', which many European politicians and debaters have warned against, will have a more fertile ground if Muslim minorities are marginalised socio-economically and have to suffer prejudiced criticism.

The Muslim mainstream, which has also been referred to as the silent majority of Islam, is used here as a designation for those Muslims whose beliefs and practices are strongly influenced by various local traditions from their predominantly Muslim countries of origin. These may differ substantially from what according to Islamists and other more 'orthodox' Muslims characterises 'true' Islam. For example, Muslims from the countryside in Turkey often believe in the 'evil eye' as a cause of disease and other kinds of misfortune. In comparison to Islamists, mainstream Muslims tend to be somewhat less interested in the idea of Islam as an ideology and a political system. Also, they are less strict in terms of observing, for instance, the daily prayers (*salat*) and the fasting of Ramadan. The prohibition of alcohol is not always followed. However, the prohibition of pork is a symbolically important issue for the great

majority of Muslims and therefore observed by almost everyone.
Thus, even secularised people with a Muslim – or Jewish – background avoid eating pork products.

It seems likely that the present mainstream will eventually be
replaced by Euro-Islam as the majority position, which would thus
form the new mainstream. Euro-Islam, which has become a quite
common concept, refers to the more or less conscious striving to
contextualise Islam in Europe. Every religion is, unavoidably,
influenced by the cultural and religious environment in which it
develops. It is largely a question of unconscious inculturation, to use
a concept that is common in Christian discussions of mission
milieus, but it is also an issue of very conscious attempts at contextualisation. In Europe it is particularly Muslims of the second
and third generations who work for the development of European
forms of Islam. This striving may concern everything from views on
mosque architecture and dress to theological issues regarding
Muslim views on science, environmental policies and the relationship between Muslims and Christians or people of other faiths. The
role of women and gender relations are issues of particularly lively
debate. Much of the theological renewal within Islam today is found
among European and American Muslims. Considering the fact that
Western Muslims, compared to people in predominantly Muslim
countries, are exposed to the challenge of modern Western cultures
in a more direct way, this is hardly surprising.

How, then, does Sufism relate to the various types of Islam that
have been outlined above? As there are Sufis within both Sunnism
and Shiism, as well as in all the different law schools, there are Sufi
Muslims representing all these types of Islam in Europe. A small
minority of Sufis have become secularised. Others, who form another
small minority, are influenced by Islamist ideas and stress the
significance of the exoteric and legal aspects of Islam. The majority
of Sufis belong to the mainstream. It is largely through Sufism that
Islam has spread to new parts of the world and Sufi Muslims usually
show a flexible capacity for integration in such areas.

Sufis may take part, for instance, in prayer services in mosques
together with Muslims who are not Sufis, but they also have their
own gatherings centred around *dhikr* ('remembrance', often
repetitions of the names of God). In studies of Sufism in a Western

setting it is particularly important to differentiate between Islam-oriented and more universalistically focused forms of Sufism. A universalistic and eclectic orientation has deep roots in Sufism, but it finds a particularly fertile ground in contemporary Western contexts. Although the majority of Sufis have a clear Islamic identity, there are a growing number of Sufi Muslims who have a generally religious rather than an exclusively Islamic view of life. Like secularised people with a Muslim background, some universalistically oriented Sufis form a category that is basically outside Islam. For the modern development of universal forms of Sufism, European Sufi leaders have played an especially important role; and with regard to leaders as well as to the contents of their message it may be appropriate to speak of a form of Euro-Sufism. Because of its universalism this form of Sufism, which will be exemplified in this chapter, crosses the borders of Islam and enters into several other fields of religion.

Panorama

Sufism has always been a multiplex phenomenon. Among other things, this is because of the (bigger or smaller) distance from 'orthodox' forms of Islam, the continuous development of different orders and the previously stressed ability of flexible adaptation to new environments. While there has been an emphasis on the esoteric or inner side of religion, the exoteric or outer forms have varied greatly. The variety that characterises Sufism in Africa and Asia is a characteristic of its development in Europe too. All the main orders, as well as several smaller ones, have been 'exported' to Europe by Muslim immigrants. In addition, new branches have evolved in this part of the world. France is often mentioned as the European country with the strongest Sufi presence, but also in the country that once had an even larger colonial empire, i.e. Great Britain, there are a very significant number of Sufi orders and other forms of Sufism. Some scholars even argue that the Barelwi tradition from South Asia, which is imbued with Sufism, is the branch of Islam in this country that has the highest number of adherents. Here, as in other European countries, however, more research is needed in order to provide a more solid portrait of the significance of Sufism.

In many predominantly Muslim countries, Sufi orders and sheikhs play important political, economic and social roles. Several of the functions they have there, for example in local political bodies or as employers in healthcare and education, are, in the 'strong societies' of Europe, managed instead by public, tax-financed institutions. This entails important changes for Sufi immigrants here. Some of the societal functions of the orders may cease completely, but in several ways the Sufi involvement in 'non-religious' matters can continue. For instance, the healing activities of sheikhs, particularly in popular Sufi circles, can be regarded as an important complement to the bio-medical healthcare provided by hospitals and clinics. A tendency towards privatisation or individualisation is a general feature of Islamic change in European contexts, where religion is regarded as a sphere or dimension that is separate from other aspects of society. Thus Sufism and other forms of Islam by necessity will have a somewhat different function here than in Muslim-dominated countries in the 'third world'.

In the following sections some important examples of both traditional orders and, in particular, new movements initiated by Europeans who have become Sufis will be highlighted. One of the biggest and most widely spread orders, which is strongly represented in Europe, is the Naqshbandi. It was founded in Central Asia in the fourteenth century by Baha al-Din Naqshband, and is frequently depicted as law-oriented, meditative and strongly focused on missionary endeavours. However, there are significant differences between different branches of this order. Naqshbandi followers, who are primarily immigrants from Asia and secondarily converts, can now be found in virtually all parts of Europe. A branch that is of particular interest in the European context is the Naqshbandi-Haqqani, whose grand sheikh Muhammad Nazim al-Haqqani from Cyprus has initiated a significant number of converts since the early 1970s. Since Nazim is also the grand mufti of Cyprus, i.e. a leading authority on issues of Islamic law, Turkish Cypriots, many of whom have emigrated to European countries, form a particularly substantial group of disciples, although many people of other ethnic backgrounds see him as their master too. Important financial support is provided by the Sultan of Brunei, who is one of Nazim's followers. The Haqqani branch of the Naqshbandi order differs from more traditional branches partly in that the silent *dhikr* service is complemented by other noisy gatherings.

Another order that has attracted a fair number of European converts is the Nimatullahi, which was founded in the fourteenth century by Shah Nimatullah Wali. He was born in Aleppo in Syria but lived for many years in Iran. Nimatullahi is a Shiite order and it still has a strong position in Iran. However, its members are found in many other parts of the world too. In Europe most of the followers are people from Iran who have gone into exile. The order is well known, among other things, because of its prominent poets and prose writers. Nimatullahi sheikhs and disciples pay much attention to self-reflection. In connection with the Islamist assumption of power in 1979, the leader, Jawad Nurbakhsh, a distinguished psychiatrist who had studied both in Teheran and at the Sorbonne, and several other sheikhs were forced into exile. In 1983 Nurbakhsh took up his abode in London, where the Nimatullahi order now has its European centre.

Above all due to immigrants from various parts of Africa, orders like the Qadiriyya, Tijaniyya, Muridiyya, Ahmadiyya-Idrisiyya and Shadhiliyya, as well as some sub-divisions of these, have become established in Europe. The last-mentioned one in particular has attracted European converts who have become very influential in the development of the part of Euro-Islam that may be referred to as Euro-Sufism. The Shadhili order is named after the North African sheikh Abu Hasan al-Shadhili, who lived in the thirteenth century. Traditionally it has been much concerned with exoteric, legal matters and has attracted many intellectuals. In particular it has been influenced by the intellectual tradition of the famous medieval Andalusian philosopher and theologian Ibn Arabi. For the development of Sufism among European converts, the Darqawi branch of the Shadhili tree, which was founded by Ahmad al-Darqawi (d. 1823), has been important. A further ramification, which has been of even greater significance for this development, is the Shadhili-Darqawi-Alawi or Alawiyya, which was initiated by Abu al-Abbas al-Alawi (d. 1934). Like Shadhiliyya, both Darqawiyya and Alawiyya have a North African origin. As early as in the 1920s, Alawi convents were founded in France and England. In both of these countries, as well as in several other parts of Europe, outstanding representatives of the Shadhili tradition in the broad sense have developed this tradition in a more or less far-reaching universalist direction, which will be exemplified below.

The Bektashi and Khalwati-Jerrahi orders are represented in Europe particularly by people of Turkish origin. Another order with strong connections to Turkey is the Mawlawi (Turk. Mevlevi), which is also present in Europe and perhaps the most well known among non-Muslims because of the concerts of its 'whirling dervishes'. Among orders that are strong in South and Central Asia and which have also established themselves in Europe the Chistiyya and the Rifaiyya, named after Muin al-Din Chisti (d. 1236) and Ahmad al-Rifai, respectively, may be mentioned. While the former are known for their interest in music and dance, the latter are called 'howling dervishes' because of their exceptionally loud *dhikr*. Sometimes even flagellation is part of the Rifai *dhikr*. Among Asian immigrants in Europe there are, moreover, adherents of the Burhani or Ibrahimi-Dasuqi order, which was founded by Ibrahim al-Dasuqi in the thirteenth century and whose name of honour was Burhan al-Din ('the proof of religion'). He lived in Egypt, and in Europe there are Africans as well as converts who are members of this order.

In the following sections some prominent European Sufi leaders with connections to various order traditions will be presented briefly. One of the most important pioneers for the introduction in the West of Eastern esoteric teachings was Georgii Gurdjieff (d. 1949). He was born in Alexandropol in Transcaucasia and his ethnic background was Greek–Armenian. During a couple of decades in the late the nineteenth and early twentieth centuries he travelled in Central Asia and the Middle East, where he was influenced by Sufi ideas, especially the Mawlawi tradition. He was also interested in theosophy. Due to his later activities in European cities like New York, Paris and London, which among other things included Sufi-inspired music and dance performances, his name became well known amongst intellectuals and 'cultural workers' in the West. Gurdjieff's combined interest in Sufism and religious traditions from the Far East can be observed also among several other European Sufi leaders, for example his Norwegian disciple Wilhelm Koren, who practises Mawlawi-inspired dance as well as Hindu meditation.

For the dissemination in Europe of an eclectic and universal-istically oriented Sufism, Gurdjieff became a front-runner. His work was partly contemporaneous with the mission in the West of the Indian Chisti-inspired Hazrat Inayat Khan. During the 1910s and 20s this Sufi leader, who preached the unity of religions and the unifying power of love, attracted a number of Western followers, mainly from the middle and upper classes. Somewhat later than Gurdjieff and Khan another pioneer with a universalistic and trans-order message, Idries Shah (d. 1996), started spreading his ideas. This prolific Sufi writer, who was influenced by, among others, Gurdjieff, was the son of an Afghan writer who had married a Scottish woman and moved to England, where Idries Shah was born and grew up. Like Gurdjieff, Shah, whose books still have high circulation figures, attracted in particular intellectuals and 'cultural workers'.

Within a somewhat different type of European Sufism the Swedish painter Ivan Aguéli (d. 1917) was a pioneer. He was initiated into the Shadhili order in Egypt in 1907. Through Aguéli, who became a *muqaddam*, i.e. authorised to initiate others, the French René Guénon also became a member of the Shadhiliyya some years later. Among these and other like-minded Europeans there was a fervent interest in Ibn Arabi. In the journal *Etudes traditionelles*, which for many years was edited by Michael Vâlsan (d. 1974) in Paris, many articles about this philosopher as well as translations of his writings were published. Behind the 'traditionalism' of Aguéli, Guénon, Vâlsan and others was the idea that several religious traditions have a common kernel and that the Sufi way is a particularly effective means of reaching the goal. In a great number of learned publica-tions, Guénon developed for a European circle of readers the idea of the ancient, ageless wisdom (*philosophia perennis*) and religion (*religio perennis*).

The perennialism taught by Aguéli and Guénon was later developed further by several other Shadhili-inspired European Sufi leaders, whose orientation, however, became somewhat varied. Two particularly well-known names are the Swiss Frithjof Schuon (d. 1998) and his follower, the British Martin Lings (b. 1914), who among other things has written a biography of al-Alawi. Schuon, who in private circles was known as sheikh Isa Nur al-Din, was a prominent author initiated in the Alawi branch who attracted small groups of disciples in several countries. Concurrently with the increasing eclecticism of his Sufi teachings, the tensions between Schuon and Guénon increased. The former experienced visions centred around Mary, the mother of Jesus, and he formed a new Alawi sub-division called Maryamiyya after her. When Schuon lived in the United States in the 1980s and 90s he also became interested in the religions of the Native American population there. This, as well as certain sexual excesses, were some of the things that towards the end of his life made him increasingly controversial and isolated.

Another Shadhili-oriented European Sufi leader who, after a first phase when he stressed the esoteric contents of Sufism, changed in a very different direction from that of Schuon is the British author and former actor Ian Dallas. He is initiated into the Darqawi branch and has the Muslim name Abd al-Qadir al-Sufi al-Darqawi. He is now strongly critical of Guénon and Schuon and their followers. Abd al-Qadir's position has become more and more strictly Islamic. After some years of work in Norwich and London he moved in the mid-1980s to Spain where he preaches the need for an Islamisation of Europe. He emphasises that the exoteric or law-oriented aspects of Islam must not be separated from Sufism. His followers are called 'murabitun', which here refers particularly to pious Sufis striving for the advancement of Islam. Abd al-Qadir and his adherents differ from many other European converts to Islam because of their conspicuous, and partly Islamist-inspired, interest in political, economical and social issues. Another law-oriented form of Sufism, with certain roots in the Shadhili-Darqawi tradition as well as in Shiite Islam, is represented by sheikh Fadhlalla Haeri, an Iraqi businessman, now based in South Africa, who is doing missionary work in the West. The type of Sufism that defuses the exoteric aspects of Islam he polemically calls 'pseudo-Sufism'. However, he stresses also the need for *ijtihad*, i.e. a new interpretation of the law. Haeri is influenced by several orders and refers to himself as a 'post-*tariqa* shaikh' – an epithet that suits many West-oriented and Western Sufi leaders.

Another person in this category, who like Haeri and al-Qadir is a successful writer, is Reshad Feild. This Mawlawi-inspired Sufi teacher, who established the Zentrum Johanneshof, a Sufi centre near Lake Vierwaldstätter in Switzerland, was previously a singer in the British pop group the Springfields as well as an antique dealer and stockbroker. A similar centre, which has been important for the development of a universalistically oriented Sufism in Germany, is Haus Schnede, idyllically situated near the Lüneburger Heide south of Hamburg. This centre was founded in 1981 by the Austrian Naqshbandi- and Burhani-initiated Stefan Makowski. For several reasons, including his openness to non-Islamic elements and the repudiation of his Sudanese Burhani grand sheikh, the centre had to be closed after some years. A few years later Makowski instead opened an independent institute in Salzburg for the furthering of and research into Sufism.

In 1996 Makowski, who is a prolific writer and nowadays readily stresses his Naqshbandi affiliation, published together with his wife Samsam Renate Makowski the book *Sufismus für Frauen* (Sufism for women). There they present, among other things, historical examples of prominent Sufi women, including sheikhs, and claim that Sufism attracts women in particular because it speaks first and foremost to the heart. Although it is usually only in quite limited contexts that gender statistics may be available, it appears that – regardless of the possible causes – the Sufi messages preached by European Sufi leaders have attracted as many, and probably more, women than men. Among Sufi leaders, however, women have so far formed a small minority. An interesting exception is sheikh Irina Tweedie, a Russian with theosophical interests, who after a couple of years of spiritual quest in India at the beginning of the 1960s started teaching in England. In 1979 she published an autobiographical book entitled *Chasm of Fire*, which in an expanded edition called *Daughter of Fire* appeared again seven years later. Here she tells about her meeting with her Indian Naqshbandi sheikh, Bhai Sahib, who was also a Hindu. At the beginning of the 1990s, when Tweedie was no longer active, her work was continued above all by Llewellyn Vaughan-Lee at the Golden Sufi Center in California, which represents a form of perennialism. His great interest in philosophy, particularly C. G. Jung, is shared by many universalistically oriented Sufi leaders in the West whose Sufism transcends the borders of Islam. In addition to North America, Tweedie's followers are also found in England, Germany and Switzerland.

A religious integration of men and women is not something completely new within Sufism. In exceptional cases this has existed for a long time, particularly in the Bektashi order, which has contributed to stern criticism from 'orthodox' Muslims. However, it is only within modern European and American Sufism that a gender integration has become common. An interesting pioneer among European Sufi women is another Russian, Isabelle Eberhardt, who in 1900, at the age of twenty-three, was initiated into the Qadiriyya in Tunisia – i.e. seven years before Aguéli became a Muslim in Egypt, even though at that time the initiation of a Western woman was an isolated event. With regard to female influence, the Sufi movement of Khan is of particular interest. His first female disciple was Rabia Martin, whom he appointed as Sufi teacher and guide (*murshida*) in the United States in 1912. In the movement initiated by Khan, women have always played an important role. He also appointed several female sheikhs. This was at a time when the issue of female ordination of Christian priests or pastors was hardly even discussed, although there have been Christian forerunners in this respect too, for instance within the Salvation Army, where from the very beginning women could be leading officers. In predominantly Muslim countries at the beginning of the twentieth century, the discussion about the possibility of having female religious leaders, such as imams, was even less topical than within Christianity in the West.

There are now a great number of European Sufis who do not formally practise Islam. Clearly, their interest in Sufism is often triggered by the reading of books written by leading European and other Sufis or by an interest in certain cultural aspects such as poetry, dance and music. The fact that many Sufi groups make frequent use of the Internet is another reason for the growing interest in Sufism. Since the Internet is inexpensive and easy to manage, even very small organisations can utilise this medium for spreading information about ideas and publications. Music and dance tours by, in particular, Mawlawi Sufis, as well as the many translations of Sufi poetry, have had a significant impact. Also, there are Sufi-inspired choirs that have produced CDs and cassettes, which are sold in the West. For example, the Qawwali music, which has its roots in the Chisti tradition, has become well-known in the

West. In some universalistically oriented Sufi groups men and women dance together. Sufi-inspired dancing may even take place in churches and therapeutic contexts without any connection to Islam.

Although there are only very small groups of people in Europe who have become Sufis, Europeans have often been more favourably disposed towards Sufism than towards more 'orthodox' forms of Islam. There has been, and still is, a tendency to see Sufism as a comparatively 'acceptable' form of Islam. The fact that Sufism has inspired intellectuals and people working in the fine arts in particular is partly because of the rich cultural Sufi heritage in terms of, among other things, philosophical thinking, music and poetry. Text-oriented work and translations of Sufi writings by European scholars and other intellectuals have contributed largely to the spreading of knowledge about Sufism. Among such people, Reynold Nicholson and Arthur Arberry in Great Britain, Louis Massignon and Henri Corbin in France as well as Annemarie Schimmel and Bernd Ratke in Germany may be mentioned. For the formation of European portraits of Sufism, the philologically and religio-historically focused studies of such intellectuals have played an important role. By contrast, newer and more ethnologically or anthropologically oriented works about Sufism in popular contexts, where Sufi texts have not been produced, have not become very well known. Many of the scholars who have carried out research on Sufism, such as Massignon and Corbin, who were both influenced by perennialist thinking, have also had a more or less favourable view towards this type of religion.

Sufi theologies of religion

Tendencies towards individualism, a striving for equality between the sexes and a focus on cultural aspects such as poetry, music and dance, which were briefly referred to above, are some of the factors that have contributed to the European interest in and positive portraits of Sufism. Another important aspect in this context is the religio-theological openness that usually characterises Sufism, particularly in Europe. This section will focus on some important examples of theologies of religion within European Sufism.

In the theology of religion there is a great difference between, on the one hand, the most exclusive and, on the other hand, the most universalistic. The term exclusivism can be used to denote the idea that the central contents of one religion only is true, and that it is only by professing this religion that the religious goal, such as salvation, liberation or enlightenment, can be achieved. For denoting the pluralistic view that basic truths are expressed in several or even all religions, the term universalism has already been used. With a historically focused terminology, one may speak about theologies of discontinuity and continuity, respectively, in order to denote a more or less exclusive theology of religion.

Traditionally, Christian theologies of religion have tended to be somewhat more exclusive than Islamic ones. According to a well-known text in the Bible (John 14: 6), Jesus once said: 'I am the way, the truth and the life. Nobody comes to the Father except through me'. Statements leaning towards an exclusivist position may be found in the Quran too. For example, in Sura 3: 85 it is said that a person who chooses a religion other than Islam will stand among the losers in the hereafter. However, in the Islamic tradition there is, in principle, an acceptance of the religions of the so-called people of the book (*ahl al-kitab*). This expression usually refers to Jews and Christians, to whom apostles before Muhammad revealed divine messages. There is a continuity from Adam, who is sometimes referred to as 'the first Muslim', and prophets like Abraham (Ibrahim), Moses (Musa) and Jesus (Isa) to Muhammad, who conveyed the final divine message, i.e. the Quran. Although Muslims argue that the people of the book have neglected and distorted certain parts of the messages entrusted to them, Muslims usually do not think that they ought to convert to Islam.

With reference to the term Sabeans, which is derived from an Arabic root that means lean against or stand close to, religions other than the 'Abrahamic', i.e. Judaism, Christianity and Islam, have been accepted by 'orthodox' religious leaders (*ulama*) too. This concerns, for example, Zoroastrianism. In exceptional cases, even Hinduism has been provided with a Muslim theological legitimation. However, in general there has been a stern dissociation from polytheistic religions, especially those that lack a scriptural tradition. Polytheism (*shirk*) is regarded as a particularly serious sin, and the monotheist message is frequently stressed. The basic creed (*shahada*), 'there is no god but God and Muhammad is His apostle', is recited, for instance, when somebody converts to Islam.

Leading biblical figures play important roles in the Quran and Islamic traditions too. Above all, the sayings about Jesus are so frequent that some scholars have written about an Islamic 'Isalogy', i.e. teachings about Jesus. He is viewed as a great apostle, born of a virgin, even though it is emphasised that he was not divine and was not killed on the Cross for the salvation of human beings. Mary (Marya), Jesus' mother, is also regarded as chosen by God and is revered by Muslims. Within Sufism, in particular, Jesus has been most important as an example to follow. Not least his morally highly advanced and ascetically focused lifestyle has been a great source of inspiration for many Muslims. The miracles that Jesus performed have inspired in particular many Sufi sheikhs for whom healing has been an important part of their activities. One – of many – Sufi writers who refers to biblical figures is Makowski. In his book *Allahs Diener in Europa* (God's servants in Europe) of 1997 he has, among other things, provided examples of Sufis in the Bible. According to him, such examples are found in particular among figures who in the Old Testament or Hebrew Bible are called prophets. Makowski devotes one chapter to Sufism for Christians and the Sufi way that, in his view, starts with Mary and Jesus.

Within Sufism there is a religio-theological span where the distance between the extreme points is longer than within more 'orthodox' forms of Islam. In order to designate the extremes of this scale, I will in the following use the above-mentioned terms exclusivism and universalism. Between the extreme points there are a great number of types of more or less pluralistic positions. There is no evident congruence between a person's views on the religious beliefs of other human beings and the way he or she treats people with other beliefs. However, the aim of this chapter is not to discuss how various intellectual or theoretical ideas are related to ethics and practices.

It is hardly possible to speak about a downright exclusivistic theology of religion within Sufism and particularly not within European Sufism, where the tendency instead is towards universalist positions. However, there are some examples of Sufis in Europe who have moved in the other direction and come close to an exclusivistic point of view. Here influences from Islamist movements with significant mission interests played a decisive role. An important example of a movement with roots in the Naqshbandi tradition that has changed in an Islamist direction and thus become more exclusivist is the Nurjuluk, which was founded in Turkey by sheikh Beidüzzaman Said Nursi (d. 1960). This movement is strong in Turkey but has many adherents among Turkish immigrants in Germany too. In Great Britain a splinter group from the World Islamic Mission, the Barelwi organisation that was first established there, has also developed in an increasingly exclusivist, Islamist direction. The new organisation, the International Islamic Organisation, was founded by sheikh Abdul Wahhab Siddiqi (d. 1994) from Coventry. He had a Naqshbandi background too, but developed cooperation with the radically Islamist Kalim Siddiqi (d. 1996), who was inspired by the Islamic Republic in Iran and formed the Muslim parliament in London, which among other things aimed at the establishment of a global Islamic state.

Perhaps the most striking example of a Sufi movement that has become increasingly exclusivistic is the previously mentioned Murabitun. Its leader, Abd al-Qadir, and his followers have more and more emphasised the need for non-Muslims to convert to Islam. Concurrently an increasing isolation from the non-Islamic, European context as well as from Muslims whose conception of Islam is regarded as too 'mixed up' with beliefs and practices from other religions has been observed. The surrounding European society is seen as 'barbaric', and there are sometimes anti-capitalistic as well as anti-democratic elements in the militant polemics of al-Qadir. In order to establish a divinely sanctioned order, Europe must be conquered by Islam, starting with a reconquest of Andalusia. Despite occasional extreme Islamist statements, however, the adherents of Murabitun have not abandoned Sufism, the 'heart' of Islam, which is said to provide Muslims with the spiritual nourishment they need.

It is interesting to note that when more or less Islamistically influenced Muslims like Abd al-Qadir make polemical utterances, it is often secular elements of Western culture rather than Christianity that they criticise. There is a form of occidentalism that depicts godlessness as a root of the great problems that Europe and other parts of the West are said to suffer from. In stereotypic pictures the West is portrayed as one-sidedly materialistic, violence-ridden, immoral and socially impoverished. The lack of divinely inspired morals leads to, among other things, accelerating criminality, prostitution, unemployment and social maladjustment. Secularism, the divide between religion and politics, is linked to European enlightenment values, which are seen as the source of many evils. However, there is also a criticism of Christianity here, since some of the roots of modern secularism are found in the New Testament and its separation of things that belong to God and those that belong to the emperor.

While it is difficult to find examples of Sufism with far-reaching exclusivist tendencies, it is easy to exemplify various standpoints which are more or less close to a clear-cut universalistic position. It can be concluded that a movement towards universalism is one of the most striking characteristics of Sufism in a European context. However, most Sufis seem to uphold the classic Islamic distinction between religions that are or those that are not 'divinely revealed', even though a considerable inclusivity characterises most Sufi interpretations of terms like people of the book and Sabeans. Thus, it is common that religions other than Judaism and Christianity are regarded as divinely legitimated. In particular, it is often stressed that the kernel of 'scriptural religions' like Hinduism, Buddhism and Zoroastrianism is true. Sometimes Chinese religions such as Taoism and Confucianism are mentioned too. By making a distinction between the kernels of religions and their outer forms, or their esoteric and exoteric dimensions, respectively, it is possible to be simultaneously affirming and polemic. Moreover, the *lack* of references to religions that lack scriptures is conspicuous. As a rule, such religions are not seen as divinely inspired.

A religio-theological position between strict exclusivism and universalism is usually represented by the main Sufi orders that have become established in Europe. The pluralist orientation is frequently strengthened in the European context. An interesting example of this is the message of the previously mentioned sheikh Nazim. He is a devout Muslim who carefully practises the outer forms of Islam and is deeply anchored in a classical Naqshbandi tradition. Yet he holds that a demand for strict adherence to the legal rules of Islam would hinder the spreading of Islam among non-Muslims. Hence he preaches the widest possible tolerance for people who convert to Islam. It is true that Nazim has reiterated the classical Islamic attitude that other religions than Judaism, Christianity and Islam are human constructions. Nevertheless, he has, for instance, visited Buddhist monasteries and been a guest at meetings in Great Britain that have been organised by Hindus. Moreover, he has argued that the differences *within* religions are more interesting than the differences *between* them, which is a common attitude among mystics, and that there are Sufi ways within all religions. Official forms of religion, managed by official leaders, such as Muslim imams and Christian priests, are often criticised sharply, and the need to search for genuine religious experiences is stressed.

The religio-theological position of the Nimatullahi sheikh Jawad Nurbakhsh is similar to that of Nazim. Thus Nurbakhsh has dissociated himself somewhat from his order's traditional emphasis on the connection between Sufism and the law (*sharia*). Rather he accentuates the need for love of everything and the universal aspects of Sufism. Human beings should be respected regardless of their religious affiliation. To a certain extent Nurbakhsh has been influenced by traditionalists who preach perennialism. In Stockholm, for instance, the local Nimatullahi leader emphasises, among other things, the significance of Jesus as a perfect master, whose message is said to be in accordance with Sufism, and that Sufi ways exist outside Islam too. His mosque in a suburb of Stockholm is open not only to initiated adherents but also to other people who may take part in *dhikr* services.

Among Sufis with a markedly pluralist orientation there are strikingly many who were born and bred in Europe. Of particular interest is the perennialism or traditionalism which has been represented primarily by Guénon and Schuon. In Sweden the leading representative of this tradition has been the author Kurt Almqvist (d. 2001). Following Guénon and Schuon, Almqvist holds that the essence of the divine 'Unity', which can be formulated only within esotericism, the 'depth level' of religion, is inherent in all divinely revealed religions. He does not define which religions belong to this category. In addition to Islam, however, his interest is clearly focused on medieval Christianity and Eastern religions, especially Hinduism. Ideo-historically perennialism is also linked to Hermetism and Neoplatonism. Like Guénon, Schuon and other representatives of perennialism, Almqvist is very critical of the excessive materialism, one-sided rationalism and secularly inspired belief in development that is said to characterise the modern (secularised) West. As indicated above, Schuon's position was particularly far-reaching in terms of eclecticism and, among other things, his interest in the religions of Native Americans led to criticism from other representatives of the perennialist tradition. Some of them even dissociated themselves completely from him.

In his book *What is Sufism?* (1975), the perennialist Martin Lings compares the divine presence to, among other things, an endless ocean from which at various times revelations have flowed like waves to different parts of the globe. The forms of these waves have been somewhat different depending on the time and place with which they have been linked. The great majority of people are concerned only with this exoteric dimension of the divine presence, while mystics within different traditions are absorbed by the depth of the source, i.e. the ocean that has both an outer and an inner part. Lings emphasises that particularism can be combined with universalism – the differences are found in the exoteric, while the sameness belongs to the esoteric level. A merging of the particular with the universal can be seen, for instance, in sacred art. Thus a Muslim may conceive of, among other things, Hindu temples and Christian cathedrals as manifestations of the divine. According to Lings, Islam can make special claims to universalism because it restores the primordial religion; and because Sufism lays stress on the connections between Islam and other religions, it can serve as a bridge between East and West.

The thought patterns that have emerged from, in particular, Gurdjieff and Khan are in religio-theological as well as in some other aspects similar to the partly Shadhili-influenced perennialism. Thus, like Guénon, Almqvist and others, Gurdjieff and Khan accentuated the significance of the esoteric kernel of Christianity and Eastern religions like Hinduism. An important link between Gurdjieff, Khan and many of their followers is, furthermore, the theosophical influences. Sufism is conceived of as pre-Islamic and has always existed. However, *one* important branch of Sufism is found within Islam. By spreading the message about the esoteric unity of religions, it is believed that prejudices that exist among believers within various religions, with different exoteric forms, will disappear. Khan stresses that those people who have gained knowledge about the inner and higher life are no longer bound to exoteric rules but can themselves find norms that suit them.

Conclusions and final remarks

Islamism, or 'fundamentalism' within several religions, and universalism have sometimes been regarded as different reactions to globalisation. It should be remembered, however, that such thought patterns are not new but have existed at other times too, although they have become particularly important in recent decades. In Europe 'fundamentalism' is a much weaker movement than in the 'third world'. This is probably largely because in that part of the world, which has suffered from European colonialism, many people tend to conceive of globalisation as a new form of Western, and now especially American, dominance. Ayatullah Khomeini, for instance, spoke about a global 'Westoxification'. For many Muslims in previously colonised areas, Islamism may partly be seen as a genuinely indigenous self-defence, and their criticism is directed against both Western countries and their own leaders who have 'surrendered' to Western influence. Universalistic thought patterns may be said to represent a more affirming response to globalisation. When people from different cultures and religions are brought into closer contact with each other because of, among other things, increasing waves of migration and the global flow of communication, some people become influenced by religious ideas other than those they were first taught rather than working for the strengthening of their own religious tradition. The 'pick and mix' attitude that characterises the universalistically oriented forms of Sufism is also a typical feature of the broad contemporary religious current that is often referred to as 'New Age'.

In this chapter it has been shown that some Sufi groups are influenced by international Islamist currents. As a particularly evident example of this, Abd al-Qadir and the Murabitun have been highlighted. Like secularised Sufis, however, the Islamist-inspired

Sufi Muslims appear to be a small minority. A much stronger presence in Europe are those Sufis who belong to the Muslim mainstream, i.e. Sufi Muslims within traditional orders whose religious beliefs and practices are strongly influenced by different local traditions from their countries of origin, as well as those who are found within what may be called Euro-Sufism, i.e. the form of Euro-Islam that occasionally transcends the borders of Islam. The latter Sufis, who more or less consciously contextualise Sufism in the European context, form the fastest growing Sufi group and may eventually become one of the mainstays of a new mainstream of Euro-Islam.

Despite its numerical importance the present mainstream is not well known. One of the reasons for this is that Sufism in popular contexts is seldom text-producing and therefore difficult to study. In order to increase the knowledge about such Sufism more field research in local contexts is needed. Among Euro-Sufis there has for a long time existed an intellectual elite, many of whose members have published a great number of books and other publications, which has made it relatively easy to study their forms of Sufism. It is remarkable that Sufi leaders in Europe in the early twentieth century, i.e. about half a century before the large-scale Muslim emigration to this part of the world started, produced Sufi-inspired publications for a Western circle of readers. The great number of Sufi leaders who were born and bred in Europe is also notable. At the beginning of the twentieth century, Khan from India was an exception. It was not until the later part of the century, at the same time as the massive Muslim immigration, that sheikhs from predominantly Muslim countries began to play a more prominent role in Europe. Many of these, such as the Naqshbandi-Haqqani sheikh Nazim and the Nimatullahi leader Nurbakhsh, have also contributed to the growth of Euro-Sufism.

Since a universalistically oriented theology of religion has grown strong within Euro-Sufism, many Sufis in Europe, particularly converts, have adopted a generally religious rather than specifically Islamic identity. Their type of Sufism is characterised largely by individualism and, conversely, a low degree of institutionalisation, which are other similarities to the 'New Age' movement. In this chapter the striving for gender equality has been emphasised too. By way of conclusion, some other factors that may further or obstruct the establishment of Sufism in Europe will be indicated. These brief notes may also be read as a call for more research on Sufism in European contexts.

The fact that Euro-Sufism has toned down certain traditional aspects of Sufism, such as veneration of saints and some forms of healing, for instance through exorcism, which many Europeans see as 'superstition', may promote its establishment here. There are very few graves of Sufi saints in Europe, and the sacralisation of certain places, associated with saints, is unusual here too. On the whole the hierarchic distance between sheikh and disciple tends to be less conspicuous in Europe than in predominantly Muslim countries. The fact that Sufism in general, and Euro-Sufism in particular, has an apolitical tendency and often a quite limited interest in Islamic law, which tallies well with the common European concept of religion as a private matter, apparently furthers an integration too. Conversely, the stress on mysticism or the 'inside' of religion seems to be in tune with topical religious interests among Europeans, not only within the 'New Age' movement but also in churches that belong to mainstream Christianity.

The significance of the ethnic factor is difficult to assess. It is reasonable to argue that the lack of emphasis on the exoteric side of religion may make it easier for Sufis than for non-Sufi Muslims to transcend ethnic boundaries and thus gather believers with different ethnic backgrounds. Within the mainstream, however, Sufism is so closely linked to local beliefs and practices that it may be difficult for different ethnic groups to cooperate; and the limited research that has been carried out on this aspect seems to confirm that to a large degree Sufis are divided along ethnic lines in Europe too. Compared to mainstream Sufism, Euro-Sufism may have a better trans-ethnic potential. Hitherto, however, the markedly pluralistic forms of Sufism have mainly attracted converts born and bred in Europe. The kind of intellectual elitism that characterises the universalistically oriented forms of Sufism may be one of the reasons why it has not appealed to large numbers of people, especially those without higher education.

Clearly, the potential for expansion is also limited because of the idea that the divine truth is found in several religions, including the predominant religion of Europe, i.e. Christianity. It is symptomatic that more or less universalist Euro-Sufis, by contrast to Islamistically oriented Sufis like Abd al-Qadir, have been 'closet Sufis' rather than active missionaries. While the low degree of institutionalisation may be an advantage in a context where the majority of people conceive of religion as a private matter, it can render the striving for social solidarity more difficult. Without strong lobby groups it can also be difficult to influence politicians and bureaucratic decision-makers to create conditions that are conducive to the group.

Finally, it may be argued that, even though Sufism in Europe may be regarded as a relatively 'acceptable' form of Islam, it can easily become the victim of 'guilt by association'. It is likely that the great majority of Europeans have a very limited knowledge of Sufism and may have problems in differentiating one form of Islam from another. The fact that some European, and particularly American, politicians after the fall of the Soviet empire in 1989 and the terrorist attack on the World Trade Center in September 2001 have begun to see Islam as the 'great threat' has not facilitated the situation for Sufis and other Muslims in Europe. It is now common in Europe and North America to speak about the Judeo-Christian tradition. Despite its close affinity to this tradition, Islam is usually excluded from this religious kinship, and at least in a short-term perspective it seems unlikely that the talk about the Judeo-Christian will be replaced by statements about the Abrahamic tradition or something similar. As indicated in this chapter, however, such talk – and more – is not unfamiliar to Sufis!

3

WHAT'S AMERICAN ABOUT AMERICAN SUFI MOVEMENTS?

Marcia Hermansen

What's American about American Sufi movements? On initial consideration, this question seems most likely to be posed from a European comparativist perspective. After all, someone from the Muslim world, say Egypt or South Asia, would be likely to think of the West as an undifferentiated whole. At the same time, Sufi movements that are essentially 'transplants' of orders active in Muslim countries and retain the same clientele and language among immigrants in the United States or Europe might not be thought of as significantly 'Western' at all. However, other Sufi movements that have made substantial adjustments to a new context and attract larger numbers of Europeans or North Americans are more likely to be seen as generically 'Western'. Once one starts to consider these Western Sufi movements more closely, a category of specifically 'American' Sufi movements emerges as both informative and inadequate. It is informative in the sense that movements with significant activities based in the United States do adapt styles and practices resonant with American ways of doing things. It is inadequate with respect to the impossibility of drawing a line between the United States and Europe and imagining no cross-fertilisation and circulation of leaders, members and publications of particular groups, even more so in an age of electronic communication and Internet linkages. Therefore, in viewing the situation of contemporary American Sufi movements, we need to consider both transnational theory and activity and those factors which exhibit local, regional and particular contextual influences.

In the following discussion I will consider American Sufism as contrasted with 'Euro-Sufism' under a set of broad issues and categories.

The role of religion in American culture

Distinctively American elements of Sufi movements in the United States may be broadly related to aspects of American religious and cultural practice and identity. In his social and political study of the United States, *Democracy in America* (1961 edn), Alexis de Tocqueville who visited in 1831 wrote, 'the religious atmosphere of the country was the first thing that struck me on arrival in the United States' (p. 295). Tocqueville was impressed by the number of American denominations, by their mutual toleration, and by the focus on morality pervading American religion.

At the beginning of the nineteenth century the focus of American religion shifted from the doctrinal particulars of the various denominations to the moral character of the believer. While nineteenth-century America contained a large number of Protestant sects and denominations, all with different doctrines, practices and organisational forms, by the 1830s almost all of these bodies had developed a deeply evangelical emphasis. According to historian David Scott, Protestantism has always contained an important evangelical strain, but it was in the nineteenth century that a particular style of evangelicalism became the dominant form of spiritual expression. What above all else characterised this evangelicalism was its dynamism and the pervasive sense of activist energy it released. A major element of nineteenth-century evangelicalism in America became the experience of conversion as a dynamic religious awakening motivating to activism.

Scholars of American religion have also noted the importance and effect in the nineteenth century of movements that incorporated experiential and esoteric dimensions of the sacred, including Christian Science, theosophy and transcendentalism. Transcendentalism questioned established cultural forms, and called for a reintegration of spirit and matter. It desired to turn ideas into concrete action and spread from the original arenas of religion and education to literature, philosophy and social reform. By the twentieth century, typical Protestant concern with mastery and control was challenged and in some cases supplanted in the United States by mystical strands of letting go, feeling and experiencing. While this experiential drive was in some cases channelled back by Protestant (or Catholic) denominations into revitalising movements within the church, an increasing number of Americans became unaffiliated or rejected mainline Christianity as too being dull.

The popularity of Sufi movements in the late twentieth century represents one consequence of the attraction of Americans to experiential modes of spirituality, and indicates a new readiness to cross boundaries and abandon previous affiliations.

According to an expert on American Protestantism, Martin Marty, traditional denominations and congregations hold the loyalty of about 40 per cent of Americans actively and 60 per cent passively year in year out. What has changed over the last half century is the fluidity of boundaries as multi-culturalism and pluralism prevail as the national consensus. Another acute observer of contemporary religious life in America, Wade Clark Roof, sees American religious style as increasingly embracing the spiritual. In a survey conducted by him, more than 60 per cent of younger American respondents indicated that other religious teachings should be explored. This sets out another broad context for the receptivity, although limited, to Sufism among the American population at large.

Roof summarises some characteristics of what he calls the 'seekers' among American 'baby boomers', as opposed to other individuals in this same cohort who remain connected to a community of memory and retain their childhood religious affiliations. This 'seeker' baby boomer cohort, the most important one represented in American Sufi movements, is characterised by Roof as individualistic and knowledge-oriented. Such individuals are mentally mobile and lack rootedness leading to their 'metaphysical loss of home'. In response, 'seekers' often move from one religious practice or group to another. Many participants in American Sufi movements from this cohort have already experimented with other spiritual movements and many remain comfortable with a degree of spiritual eclecticism. In religion, Wade observes, the seekers' drive for experience is more important than the epistemological cogency of teachings with which they may experiment.

Americans are said to be the most religious among the Western industrialised nations on the basis of responses to survey items such as reporting belief in God or religious experiences. Religion in America is characterised as being individual rather than institutional, and shaped by voluntarism, individual choices of loyalty and allegiance. American civil values that translate into religious attitudes are love of liberty, democratic equality and the separation of church and state. Resonant with the spirit of liberty and voluntarism is individualism, so that religion becomes a choice, a personal therapy, something attained by 'design' which may be encountered and selected on the basis of promotion, leading to its association with consumption, commodification and advertising.

Catherine Albanese, a noted historian of American religion, uses the idea of American activism to elicit distinctive cultural features of American religiosity. She theorises that American activism translates into a religious style that puts a premium on public and expressive behaviour, and in addition encourages simplification of doctrine and practice. She observes that contemporary Americans are very busy, they generally have little time for thought, and they want quick results achieved through practical technologies. The energetic style typical of American culture is expressed in the love of the automobile and speeding, in the prevalence of fast food outlets, and in a preference for all things 'lite', including religious demands. Rootlessness and rebelliousness typify religion and culture in this land of immigrants. A 'New World' country born out of 'revolution' often leads to ahistorical perceptions of religion. The following observations on American Sufism will reprise some of these themes.

Immigration history and patterns

An important feature of American Sufi movements is their diversity. In an earlier essay I used the metaphor of a garden in which there are perennials, hybrids and transplants in order to indicate the nature of this variety. The perennial and hybrid Sufi movements are ones which have made more adjustments to the American context in terms of practice and style and whose followings are dominated by Caucasian and African Americans, rather than first-generation immigrants. At the same time, I feel that the nature of immigration and the perception of immigrants are important to the character of all American Sufi movements and thus I will commence with that category.

Since immigration is the context of much of the Muslim experience in America, some discussion of the history of the Muslim presence is appropriate to set the stage for this topic. Scholars of Muslim immigration to the United States have proposed models of stages or waves characterised by diverse concerns, ethnic backgrounds and religious attitudes. A synopsis of this model is that there have been some five stages of Muslim immigration to America. The first wave, in the late nineteenth century up to World War I, was composed mostly of uneducated and unskilled young people from the rural areas of what now constitutes Syria and Lebanon, then under Ottoman rule. According to Adair Loomis and Yvonne Haddad in *Islamic Values in the United States* (1987), opportunities such as those offered by Detroit and the automobile factories attracted both Arab Christians and Muslims. The second wave of Muslim immigrants, 1918–22, followed World War I. By the time of the third wave, 1930–8, American laws confined immigration primarily to relatives of those already in the country who were naturalised citizens. In the early years of Muslim immigration, institution-building was minimal since many Muslim immigrants perceived themselves to be temporary sojourners rather than permanent settlers.

Following World War II, Muslim immigrants included displaced groups from Eastern Europe fleeing Communism, as well as children of the educated elites in various Arab countries and South Asia who were mostly urban in background, educated and Westernised prior to their arrival in the United States. These immigrants often came in pursuit of higher education or career opportunities. It is this cohort that founded many of the more permanent Muslim institutions in America, for example the Islamic Society of North America (ISNA) and the first chapters of the Muslim Student Association.

The change of immigration laws in the mid-1960s opened the doors to what might be considered a fifth wave, although diverse backgrounds and causes for immigration characterise these later Muslim immigrants. The wars and upheavals of this period gave rise to their own ethnic waves of immigrant Iranians, Afghans, Somalians, Bosnians and so on.

In addition to these immigrant populations, a significant proportion of the Africans brought to the New World as slaves may have been Muslim. In any event, today the large numbers of 'indigenous' African American converts to Islam gives the broader Muslim community a distinct character in that it is both immigrant and convert-based.

The population of Muslims in the United States is more diverse than that of most individual European nations, which tend to have experienced patterns of immigration from particular regions due to linguistic, historical and legal reasons. As in Europe, most Muslim immigrants settle in urban areas and chain migration is a common pattern. The number of Muslims in the United States is a matter of some discussion, and the current estimate of roughly six million indicates that Muslims will become the largest non-Christian minority religion there sometime during the next decade.

The three major groups of Muslims in the United States are African American (indigenous) Muslims, Arab Muslims, and South Asian Muslims. One estimate puts African Americans at 42 per cent, South Asians at 24.4 per cent, and Arabs at 12.4 per cent (with smaller groups of Africans at 6.2, Iranians at 3.6, South East Asians at 2, European Americans at 1.6, and 'other' at 5.4 per cent). Another estimate puts 'Americans' at 30, Arabs at 33 and South Asians at 29 per cent.

Due to the diversity of ethnic origin, no single Muslim country has influence over the American Muslim population. While the Saudis have funded certain mosques and organisations, their institutional influence is less direct than, for example, that of Turkey on migrants in Germany. The major American Muslim organisations such as ISNA and ICNA (Islamic Circle of North America) have traditionally been heavily dominated by proponents of international Muslim activist movements such as Jamaat Islami or Ikhwan al-Muslimun. This is probably due to the predominance of educated professionals among their membership who had espoused such views in their own societies in the Middle East and South Asia. The relevance of this to our argument is the fact that, since these groups favour a more literalist interpretation of Islam and reject Sufism, mystical influences were generally kept out of their organisations.

The United States, in contrast to Britain and France, had not been a direct colonial power. Therefore the status of immigrants from Muslim societies and their educational background and language skills tended to be higher, since the immigration process was relatively selective. This means that many Muslim immigrants occupied high-status professions such as medicine or engineering within the first generation and became a 'model minority'. This affected both the type of Islamic practices approved by the main body of Muslims in the United States and their perception of popular Sufi practices and doctrines as being superstitious innovations.

A European researcher, N. Landman, noted the distinction in the Netherlands between the style of popular Islamic practices brought with them by immigrants and the more intellectual and elitist Sufism which attracts Westerners to Islam. The situation is similar in the American context. In addition, the tendency of Muslim immigrants to the United States to arrive with higher educational and class backgrounds results in their often disassociating themselves from popular Islamic religious practices. The transplantation of South Asian pirs and their disciples, as has occurred in the British midlands, is therefore absent from the American Sufi scene. It is only recently that Sufism has been allowed any profile within organisations such as ISNA, in terms of their allowing speeches which refer to Sufism in coded language such as *akhlaq* (ethical theory), *ihsan* (spiritual beautification) or *tazkiyya al-nafs* (purification of the soul), including in their annual bazaar booths sponsored by 'sober', immigrant-based Sufi organisations.

The identity of the United States as a homeland for immigrants is clear from the prominent symbolism of the inscription of the Statue of Liberty: 'Give me your tired, your poor, your huddled masses yearning to breathe free, the wretched refuse of your teeming shore. Send these, the homeless, tempest-tost to me, I lift my lamp beside the golden door'. More recently, the earlier metaphor of America as a melting pot has been re-examined and displaced in favour of the idea of a salad bowl in which each element retains its original flavour but contributes to a whole greater than the sum of its parts.

Within this salad bowl, Muslim immigrants as a later addition to the mix are often characterised as adopting one of three principal attitudes: as contributors, assimilationists and rejectionists. Aside from this ethnic mix imagery, American Sufi movements, since they involve more indigenous Americans and second-generation immigrants, may be viewed as either hybrids or bridges between the two communities or deviants from both.

American converts and Sufi orders

A cultural process of gradualism and hybridisation occurs when Islamically oriented Sufi movements attract significant numbers of Americans and Canadians and make adjustments such as gradualism in Islamic practice as part of broadening their appeal. Gradualism always was a factor of conversion in Muslim expansion. Some might term it Islamisation, and it clearly does not happen overnight.

The role of conversion to Islam in American society, I would suggest, is distinctive. Conversion is, on the whole, more socially acceptable in the United States than in Europe since the imagery, vocabulary and history associated with 'turning Turk' is absent. Religion in America is voluntary, a lifestyle choice, and not as directly linked with ethnicity. The African American element in society also domesticates Islam in the public sphere, and the image of the Muslim as enemy, while certainly present, especially due to the wider Middle Eastern conflicts and terrorist attacks, is complicated by Islam's association with an important strand of American culture. Islam is often portrayed as a religion of racial harmony, for example in the autobiography of Malcolm X or in the conversion of Muhammad Ali into an American hero. The idea of transcending racial identity and espousing a progressive stance on race is resonant with many converts to Islam, black and white, and thus present in American Sufi movements. Some Sufi movements such as the Guru Bawa Fellowship and the Naqshbandi-Haqqani order, are especially racially integrated, whereas the more perennial or New Age movements tend to appeal primarily to Caucasians, who adopt fewer distinctive symbols, such as names and dress codes, of specifically Muslim identity.

During recent crises, American Sufi movements have increasingly taken on the role of representing the 'good' Muslims. Evidence for this would be the courting of the political establishment by Sheikh Hisham Kabbani of the Naqshbandi-Haqqanis: for example, his meeting with the Clintons featured on the cover of the *Muslim Magazine*, his participation in a State Department briefing and the copious Naqshbandi web page citations regarding such activities. The high level of interfaith participation by Sufis also indicates their place on the front line of public relations initiatives for a positive image of Islam in the United States.

American style: commodification, gradualism and advertising

One distinctive feature of America is its identification as a producer of great wealth and a consumer-oriented culture. The metaphors associated with religious diversity in America range from a spiritual smorgasbord, a 'divine deli', to a rational choice-based marketplace in which religions compete for market shares. The nineteenth-century French observer of American democracy and religion, Alexis de Tocqueville, observed how the importance of worldly prosperity had all but displaced concern with otherworldly salvation in American religious discourse. Thus this prominence of economic concern is nothing new.

However, we should not ignore the fact that in its traditional homelands Sufism was an important social institution as well as a set of normative beliefs and practices. Land grants, clientage, support networks, lobbying at court and the charismatic support of dynasties and the political system were all part of Sufi activities. Therefore it is not surprising that some engagement with economic factors will be part of American Sufi activities, albeit condemned by certain Sufi orders or theorists. Our task is to evoke what might be 'American' in style or substance.

One such element is the trend towards promotion and advertising. Sufi movements in the United States want to be visible to prospective recruits and therefore they employ vehicles such as lectures, seminars and conferences. Unlike more aggressive new religious movements such as the Hari Krishnas, they do not proselytise in airports and other public spaces; rather they hope to attract those who are already seeking.

Some observers, such as the French writers Lisbeth Rocher and Fatima Charqaoui, have suggested that there is an 'American' quality to some Sufi activities taking place in the United States. These include fondness for public performance, extensive use of media such as computer networks, exploitation of radio and newspaper coverage, and Sufi dancing, contrasting with a more sober and retiring attitude on the part of Sufi orders operating in Western Europe.

Admiration of the thirteenth-century Sufi poet Rumi, especially for the translations of his work by Coleman Barks, have propelled his writings to best-selling status and garnered the admiration of icons of American pop culture such as the New Age doctor Deepak Chopra and the pop star Madonna. Both of these individuals were featured in a TV documentary promoting Rumi's values. In addition, American Sufi orders sponsor an annual Rumi festival in North Carolina which is attended by representatives of various American Sufi groups and other interested participants.

In particular, the followers of Sheikh Hisham have sought and attracted media attention ranging from the 'Sufi's Choice' newspaper story accompanying his appearance in Montreal, Canada, to televised coverage of his first Islamic Unity Conference on the cable television channel, C-Span, to the controversial public and widely publicised statements made by him that most American mosques were controlled by extremists.

Sufi networking

In the American context, networking and cooperation among certain orders is another prominent feature. This may in part be due to the circulation of a certain cohort among spiritual movements and the fact that seekers often shift allegiances from one movement or teacher to another. The idea of shopping for teachers or experiences may be illustrated by Sufi conferences and seminars where presenters, paid or volunteer, present themselves to an audience interested in Sufi teachings. After the more structured presentations, opportunities are provided to meet individually or in small groups with such teachers, to 'check them out' in more detail.

Tracing such connections over time is possible through book endorsements, narratives, and oral histories of participants in Sufi movements. For example, the narrative and book endorsements from *Women Called to the Path of Rumi* (2001) by Shakina Reinhertz indicate connections among the American Mevlevis, the International Association of Sufism (Nahid Angha), the Golden Sufi Center (Irena Tweedie/Llewellyn Vaughan-Lee), the Dances of Universal Peace Movement, the poet Coleman Barks and the Inayat Khan Sufi Movement. In fact, most of these affinities date back to the 1960s and early 70s when many of Samuel Lewis's disciples agreed to follow Pir Vilayat Khan after the former's death, and many of the Sufi order initiates began to make contacts with Turkish Mevlevis and Helvetis in Turkey. As a practice, the turning (whirling) of the Mevlevis resonates with the embodied nature of the 'work' or practices of some of the universal Sufi movements, for example the spiritual walks developed by Samuel Lewis.

The seminar or workshop format is a feature of American New Age movements and could even be related to the first Parliament of the World's Religions in Chicago in 1893. Among Sufi conferences held recently, of note are the Unity conferences of Sheikh Hisham, the International Association of Sufism Conferences held annually since 1994, and smaller meetings such as those organised by Zia Inayat Khan as the 'Meeting of the Five Sheikhs' in 2000. The two latter are distinctively American in gathering diverse teachers, both male and female, and featuring Sufi teachers advocating a range of *sharia* adherence. The range of American Sufi networking extends as far as the Islamic conferences sponsored by the Nation of Islam under Louis Farrakhan, which have featured a large American Sufi contingent. My assessment is that this participation has resulted from an affinity of the self-development aspect of the Nation's teachings to American Sufism, personal contacts in the American Sufi community of the Chicago-based Sufi Sheikh Ahmad Tijani, a close adviser to Louis Farrakhan, and the paucity of mainstream Muslim leaders willing to publicly endorse Farrakhan's movement through presence at his meetings.

Sufi travel and globalisation

Travelling has been a perennial feature of the spiritual quest and a common motif of classical Sufi theory. Postmodern critics such as Gilles Deleuze and Zygmund Bauman suggest a movement from 'pilgrimage' to 'nomadism' to 'tourism' as emblematic of these times. The American Sufis I am focusing on do not have the same diasporic imagination as those of immigrant *tariqas*. Their sacred geography, however, is likewise shaped by postmodern realities. The trope of pilgrimage in search of the authentic is strong. While the 1960s and early 70s were times for the nomadism of Western youth searching for authenticity in Eastern spiritualities and sites, more recently this seeking has been framed as Sufi tourism. Some notable examples are the Shambhala tour of Turkey (2001) proposed by Carl Ernst and Kabir Helminski (note the confluence of publishing, travel and Sufism) and the Naqshbandi-Haqqani peace tour of Central Asia (2001).

Sufi psychologies

In terms of sheer volume, a major theme of the literature inspired by American Sufi movements is concentrated in discussions of psychological models of transformation and healing. Religious life in America, with its individualism and stress on worldly results, has long incorporated dimensions of self-help and positive thinking as a means of giving the person control over his or her experiences, if not over the environment itself.

Within this typically American 'therapeutic' approach to religion, the parallelism between the Sufi sheikh and the Western psychotherapist as noted in the literature has long been recognised, as has the usurpation of the prerogatives of traditional healers and teachers by the psychologist and psychiatrist in modern Western secular culture. American Sufis often choose to contribute to this aspect personally, by being or becoming therapists; institutionally, by sponsoring conferences and forming organisations for 'Sufi psychology'; and in written form, whether formally accredited or not. The clientele of American Sufi movements who are seekers of spirituality naturally also take a strong interest in contemporary psychological approaches to personal growth, especially those of humanistic and transpersonal psychology. Idries Shah and Vilayat Khan are two perennialist Sufis who are conversant with psychotherapeutic discourse and who contribute to it at some level. In addition, attempts to bridge Islamic and contemporary psychological models have been made by the Western-trained and America-based psychologists Reza A. Arasteh, Muhammad Shafii and Laleh Bakhtiar.

Both temporally and spatially, transpersonal or third-wave psychology and Western Sufi movements have similar trajectories, dispersals and pilgrimage routes. The 1960s and 70s marked the rise of both phenomena, the San Francisco Bay area being especially prominent. The third-wave psychology movement accepted a plethora of approaches to human transformation and espoused general models that constructed Eastern meditative techniques and esoteric teachings within the 'Western' monotheisms as accomplishing the same results.

Among American Sufi movements, the complexities within transpersonal approaches engender a number of competing models of levels of the transpersonal and for cultivating consciousness. One may distinguish between psychologies that are directly 'inspired' by Sufi spirituality and psychologies versus holistic therapeutic techniques that have their origins outside the Sufi tradition but are made use of by American Sufi practitioners because they are viewed as consistent with or complementary to Sufi interest in personal transformation and healing. The latter would include Jungian psychology, the various transpersonal psychologies (e.g. Ken Wilbur, Charles Tart, Robert Ornstein, etc.) and the more recent 'soul' psychologies (e.g. James Hillman and Thomas Moore). All have in common the idea that human beings must find a way to be in touch with and live in harmony/union with some transcendent or transpersonal source of meaning and orientation. Where they locate and how they label this source varies (e.g. how much of it is beyond and how much it is within the person). The more explicitly spiritual psychologies that see this transpersonal reality as God or the divine are probably the closest parallels to the mystical way in various traditional forms of spirituality, including Sufism.

The psychologisation of religion is not unique to North America, but it is particularly significant in the Unites States. A number of Western Sufi movements seem to espouse a sort of 'scientism' according to which their psychological understanding will ultimately be validated by scientific proofs. In fact the degree of scientism seems to be a predictive factor for how universal a movement is. Many universalist Sufi movements hold that if the basis of spiritual transformation follows the laws of physics, then it should ultimately correlate with some 'unitive' scientific model.

However, the perennialist Sufis in the tradition of Frithjof Schuon strongly reject the echoes of modernism in contemporary 'scientist' discourse and wish to 'retraditionalise' science as a sacred discipline. This approach is evident in the works of Seyyed Hossein Nasr, professor and notable scholar of Islam who is Schuon's spiritual successor in the American branch of the Maryamiyya *tariqa*.

A parallel to the couching of Sufi teachings in modern psychological frameworks is Donald S. Lopez's study of Western understandings of Tibetan Buddhism. Lopez states that the modern West constructed Tibetan Buddhism less as a religion than as a science. In part this is a result of the West's own requirements that esoteric knowledge conform to the expectations of regularity, predictability and control. Arguably, some Sufi psychologies follow a similar course.

The Sufi order in the West, under the direction of Pir Vilayat Khan, for a time held annual symposiums under the auspices of its Omega Institute which drew together prominent teachers in holistic healing, New Age and Eastern spirituality, and humanistic science. Each of the movements emerging from the Shah Maghsoud Angha line, the International Association of Sufism and the MTO (Maktaba Tarigha Oveysiyya) has established its own Associations for Sufi Psychology. Representatives of these movements are now teaching in American clinical psychology programmes such as the California Institute of Integral Studies and they regularly hold academic conferences under the rubric of 'Sufi psychology'.

A quotation from a book written by a member of the International Association of Sufism, Safa Ali Uwaysi (Michael Brill Newman), entitled *The Gift of the Robe* (2000) exemplifies an understanding of the role of science in proving spiritual truths: 'Towards the end of the nineteenth century, Sufism came into contact with contemporary

Western science and within some circles, Sufism began to be transformed into a practical school grounded in scientific principles.' Some examples of Western Sufi 'psychologies' are as follows.

Jungian psychology

Jungian psychology, because it incorporates a spiritual dimension and involves a more compatible approach to dream work, has had a particular following in American Sufi movements. One of Pir Vilayat's leading deputies, the therapist Atum O'Kane, compares the transpersonal and Sufi order approaches to development, especially in the field of spiritual guidance. These include an expanded vision of the personality as an instrument for manifesting the Universal Self or divine qualities, and the specific practices of the Sufi order including meditation, breathing practices, *wazifa* (litanies), *dhikr* (recitations), light practices, creative imagination and sacred music. The volume *Sufism, Islam and Jungian Psychology* (1991), edited by J. Marvin Spiegelman, features contributions by a range of Western Sufi teachers espousing a Jungian approach, including representatives of the Sufi order (Pir Vilayat Khan, Atum O'Kane and Tasnim Fernandez), and the Golden Sufi Center (Irina Tweedie, William Dorst and Llewellyn Vaughan-Lee – all European).

Eclectic work, body work, dance, channelling

The Sufi Islamia Ruhaniat Society stemming from the teachings of Samuel Lewis (d. 1971) is particularly eclectic in using psychological and therapeutic models, especially humanistic and third-wave ones. An important quality of their practice is embodiment or body work, from Sufi dancing (the Dances of Universal Peace) to special spiritual walks and breathing techniques.

The Sufi dance movement was inspired by Samuel Lewis based on 'traditional practices of the Middle East', although in its current form it seems rather more reminiscent of folk dancing or round dancing. Unlike regular folk dances, Sufi dancing incorporates meditation, periods of focusing on sound, vibration or 'attuning' to one's own centre or to the moods and symbols evoked in the chants and dances. The purpose of the dances is both 'moral development' and 'psychic purification'. Most of the dances are performed in concentric circles with musicians and a 'caller' or leader standing in the middle. The dancers perform simple movements, turning, swaying back and forth and expanding and contracting the circles. The leader introduces the chants that accompany the dances, explaining how the symbolism of the movements corresponds to the meaning of the chants which may come from a variety of the world's religions. Examples are, 'La ilaha illa Allah' from the Islamic 'Kalima' (profession of faith) dance, 'Hare Krishna Hare Rama' from Hinduism, 'Kyrie Eleison' from Christianity and 'Shema Yisrael' from Judaism. There are supposed to have been 2,000 dances of which 200 are still commonly practised.

The Sufi dance movement has spread worldwide, far beyond the San Francisco Bay area and the initial group of 'Sufi' Sam's disciples to church groups and people who work in therapeutic and other social service organisations. Dance teacher workshops are regularly held and an individual can receive a certificate for being a 'mentor teacher'. Members of Pir Vilayat Khan's organisation, the Sufi order, also practice these dances since the Sufi Islamia Ruhaniat Society disciples of Samuel Lewis were very active in that order in the early 1970s. At that time, as his own health worsened, Lewis told his disciples to join Pir Vilayat's movement and accept his leadership, Lewis having been a student of Hazrat Inayat Khan in 1923. Lewis also created a repertoire of 'spiritual walks' which foster attunement to the planets, prophets, elements and so on, and involve the imaginative use of pacing, breath and movement in order to evoke a mood and instill permanent qualities in the practitioner.

An autobiographical reminiscence by the late successor to Samuel Lewis, Moineddin Jablonski (d. 2001), describes some types of therapeutic models and approaches used by members of this movement which are multi-religious (Sufi and Zen) and therapeutically eclectic.

Enneagram

For some time Sheikh Hisham Kabbani has claimed that his Sufi order, the Naqshbandi, had originated the Enneagram. This Enneagram movement, a sort of personality-type psychology, had become increasingly popular, particularly among groups involved in spiritual guidance, including many Catholic organisations. Sheikh Hisham's follower, Laleh Bakhtiar, has published extensively on the Enneagram and moral healing, and she and the sheikh offer seminars to therapists and New Age conferences on Sufism and the Enneagram work.

Traditional Islamic formulations using the idea of levels of the soul (nafs model)

The leader of one branch of the American Helveti-Jerrahi order, psychologist Ragip (Robert) Frager, in *Heart, Self, and Soul* (1999), makes the following comparison between Sufi and Western concepts of the person:

> The three central concepts in Islamic/Sufi Psychology are the heart, the self and the soul. Each of these technical terms has a different connotation than its common English usage and meaning. The origin and basis of these terms is Quranic and they have been expounded upon by centuries of Sufic commentaries.

In Sufic psychology the heart refers to the spiritual heart or *qalb*, not the physical organ. It is this spiritual heart that contains the deeper intelligence and wisdom (p. 2).

> The heart holds the divine spark or spirit within each one of us. It is the place of gnosis, or spiritual knowledge. The Sufic ideal is to develop a soft, feeling, compassionate heart, and to develop the heart's intelligence. This is a deeper and more grounded intelligence than the abstract intelligence of the head. It is said that when the eyes of the heart open, we can see beyond the superficial exterior of things, and when the ears of the heart open, we can hear the truth behind the words.

Frager expounds on the Sufi method of 'opening the heart' and details a spiritual, developmental theory of progress through seven stages of the self (*nafs*), and a further seven souls, which is drawn from classical Sufi theory based on Quranic terminology (pp. 47–93). He criticises some of the Western psychologies for addressing only one or two aspects of the person, not the entire range of possible development (pp. 113–14).

> Freud's description of the human being is primarily a description of the dynamics of the animal soul, in which the main motivation is to seek pleasure and avoid pain. Most of behavioral psychology focuses on the functioning of the vegetable and animal soul. Cognitive psychology deals with the mental functions of the personal soul. Humanistic psychology examines the complex activities of the human soul, such as creativity and compassion. Transpersonal psychology embraces the ego-transcending consciousness of the secret soul and the secret of secrets (soul).

This comparison of models or frameworks for transformation is congruent with Ken Wilber's model of levels of the transpersonal bands of the psyche. It should be noted that Frager is recognised as a Jerrahi sheikh and is also the director of the Institute of Transpersonal Psychology, a degree-granting institution in California.

Idries Shah and Omar Ali-Shah

The Sufi movements of Idries and Omar-Ali Shah have given some prominence to psychology in their teachings. In the United States, Shah's early deputy was Stanford University psychology professor Robert Ornstein. Shah met Ornstein in the 1960s and realised that he would be an ideal partner in the endeavour to propagate his teachings since Ornstein could cast Shah's Sufi materials into the idiom of the psycho-therapeutic community. Ornstein's book, *The Psychology of Consciousness* (1972), met with an enthusiastic reception in the academic psychology community since it coincided with the rising interest in studying bio-feedback and other techniques for shifting moods and awareness. Ornstein has continued to contribute books in this field over the years.

The reinterpretation or translation, if you will, of Sufi teachings into contemporary psychological discourses may reflect what Dale

Eickelman and Jon Anderson term a 'reintellectualisation' of Islamic discourse through presenting Islamic doctrine and discourse in accessible, vernacular terms even if this contributes to basic reconfigurations of doctrine and practice. These scholars indicate that Islamic discourse has not only moved to the vernacular and become more accessible to significantly wider publics; it has also become framed in styles of reasoning and forms of argument that draw on wider, less exclusive or erudite bodies of knowledge, including those of applied science and engineering. While this thesis was mainly formulated with respect to mass education in Muslim societies, a further dimension would include the global transformation of Sufi discourse, which is now being articulated in terms accessible to contemporary Americans.

In concluding this section on Sufi psychologies, I note that I have only been able to suggest a rather cursory outline of the frameworks and therapeutic techniques adopted by American Sufi movements. As expected, there is again a continuum from the universalist approaches to *sharia*-oriented orders. In certain orders stressing the master–sheikh interaction, the need for therapeutic models that could be generalised and applied by 'therapists as khalifas' is reduced. In other words, dispersal of charisma and limiting of personal contact with teachers encourage the construction of systematic models of transformation that can be applied irrespective of the status of the practitioner.

Sufism and American academic culture

One significant dimension of Sufism in American culture is the support it receives at the intellectual level within the academy. For one thing, religious studies as a separate field is much more common in American universities than in Europe. In the light of the constitutional separation of church and state and the pluralistic ethos of contemporary America, such departments do not promote religion per se. At the same time, approaches are often sympathetic to the religious compartment of human life, consider it significant, take the insider categories seriously or, in other words, take a phenomenological stance. Some academic institutions favour the model of the practitioner scholar who professes the religion he or she teaches.

This gives some sympathetic ground to scholars and scholarship on Sufism. The period of the late 1960s and 70s in the United States saw a convergence of larger numbers of young people interested in Eastern religions and philosophies and increased funding for graduate studies in the languages and cultures of areas of the world considered to be of strategic interest during the Cold War period. The result is a larger cohort of American academics qualified in the study of Islam and Sufism so that in the American academy the Sufi interpretation of Islam is more likely to be researched and taught, as opposed to law or Quranic studies.

The boundary between academic study and the profession of Sufism may be blurred, for instance in Seyyed Hossein Nasr's studies of Islamic spiritual themes and William Chittick's studies of Ibn Arabi and his school.

Female leadership and participation

To the degree that *sharia*-based ritual is incorporated, gender distinctions become visibly operative in the functioning of American Sufi movements. In the more strictly Islamic Sufi movements, such as the Naqshbandi-Haqqani, prominent women, if present, will likely be wives or relatives of leaders. In the case of American Sufi women, gender segregation and other restrictions on female participation are likely to provoke some discomfort, and this leads to a subversive quality in some Western women's reflections on Sufism. I mean subversive in the sense of challenging the traditional Islamic concepts of maleness and femininity and gender-specific roles.

Since I find the Turkish-originated movements of the Helveti-Jerrahis and Mevlevis interesting in terms of this theme, I will briefly introduce their movements. In the development of the Helveti-Jerrahi order in America we can see the challenges raised by negotiating both ethnic and gender identities. The order was brought to America by Sheikh Muzaffer Ozak (1914–93) of Istanbul. He first came to the United States in 1980, although many Western students of Sufism had previously visited his bookshop in Istanbul. Branches of his *tariqa* developed in New York under the leadership of Tosun Bayrak, Sheikh Nur (Lex Hixon) and in the San Francisco Bay Area under Ragip Frager.

One of the American Jerrahi leaders, Sheikh Nur al-Jerrahi (1941–95) was a prominent figure in a number of American spiritual movements. Nur (Lex Hixon) had a Ph.D. in religion from Columbia and specialised in comparative mysticism. He met Sheikh Muzaffer Ozak while the latter was a guest on a radio programme he hosted in New York where many spiritual teachers were featured. Nur eventually became his disciple and accepted Islam while maintaining his universalist orientation. The French researchers Rocher and Charqaoui, after interviewing Nur in the 1980s, marvelled that 'this gentle and affable man was an orthodox priest on Monday, a Buddhist lama on Tuesday, a Khalifa on Thursday – Christian among the Christians, Muslim among the Muslims'. This type of eclectic orientation seems to have led to some friction among members of the *tariqa* which became more evident after the death of Sheikh Muzaffer Effendi, whose successor in Istanbul, Safer Effendi (d. 1999), was said to have been more strict. Ultimately one branch of the American Jerrahis, known as the Ashkijerrahis, drawn mainly from Lex Hixon's followers, evolved separately, under a female teacher, Sheikha Fariha Fatima al-Jerrahi. One of the principal issues in the differentiation of branches among the Helvetis in America has been negotiating Islamic identity and deriving legitimacy from sheikhs based in Turkey. The branch of the Helveti-Jerrahi movement under the direction of Tosun Bayrak specifically terms itself a 'traditional Muslim Sufi order'.

The website biography of Sheikha Fariha notes that she was made a sheikha by Muzaffer Ozak in 1985 and is the first female leader in the Jerrahi order in over 300 years. More intriguingly, the biographical notice indicates that she moves through forbidden spaces while on Umra and Hajj pilgrimages in Mecca and Medina. I conclude that this reference alludes to the fact that she was able to transgress conventions of gender segregation and visit areas of the shrines normally off limits to females. Alternatively, the trope of 'forbidden spaces' resonates with escapades such as Sir Richard Burton's trip to Mecca during the 1800s. A revealing statement about identity is found on the same Ashkijerrahi website, which states that 'Islam is like clear water poured into different vessels. It takes the color and shape of each vessel'. Here Sheikh Muzaffer, who is being quoted, is said to be referring 'to both personal and cultural vessels'.

Gender issues are one measure of the adaptation of various Sufi movements to the American context. In the case of the Turkish Mevlevi order (whirling dervishes), American initiates may learn the traditional practice of 'turning' and among these disciples are American women who are set on breaking the barrier to female participation in the *dhikr*. Traditional sheikhs from Turkey may be pleased that Americans are becoming dervishes but unsettled to be asked to give permission for females to turn/whirl, at least publicly. Will different rules be negotiated for Americans?

In the book *Women Called to the Path of Rumi: The Way of the Whirling Dervish* (2001) an American female dervish reports on her experience in Turkey and her encounter with a Turkish woman (p. 172):

> I had tea with her several times after that. She thought we [American women] didn't take turning seriously. She said, 'Why would you think that you could do something that a boy starts learning to do as a very young child?' She couldn't understand how, after studying for a few years, we could go to another country and do this thing. To her it was such an American, pompous, and inflated thing to do. We continued talking, and after a while she changed her mind a bit. She could see that for me, it was an important experience. However, she still thought that I ought to be content to sit up in the balcony, because it was too hard on men who might have sexual thoughts.

Another American Mevlevi woman, cited in the same book, describing gender and other forms of equality as an ideal, states (p. 115):

> That the old, the young, black, white, male, female, all can be lovers of God, is the mystical way. This is a radical way, a way beyond control, a way that is frightening to political structures. The lover cannot be controlled. Love is a magic, which if it is truly ignited, melts slowly or quickly, our projected grids and boundaries of control upon one another.

Among the responses to the challenge raised by converted American women is activism. At the same time American Sufi women attempt to avoid the attitude which I term 'passing and surpassing', in which Euro-Americans who become Muslims receive an instant platform and prominence in Muslim contexts. In the same way that third-wave or cultural feminists try to avoid the mistake of second-wave Western white feminists who attempt to impose their agenda on women of colour, female participants in Western Sufi movements need to negotiate their understandings of gender roles to reflect both tradition and justice.

This theme is reflected in the accounts of the American Mevlevi women who were able to participate in the ritual turning or whirling in Turkey. They were sensitive to the reactions of Turkish women which were generally very positive, according to the experiences recounted in *Women Called to the Path of Rumi* (p. 114):

> All of the Turkish women who saw us were so ecstatic they had tears streaming down their faces. They had never seen men and women turn together. They had never seen women recognized in a formal *sema* [turning ritual], in a public way. To have the support to do this and also to feel all the implications of that for these Turkish women was very moving.

A recent collection of articles on Muslim women's activism in America includes pieces by two women associated with Sufi movements. Rabia Terri Harris is a member of the Helveti-Jerrahi Sufi order, the more *sharia*-oriented branch under the direction of Tohsin Bayrak. Her bio-notice says she 'came to Islam through the Jerrahi order'. Her substantial academic credentials include a BA from Princeton in religion and a Master's degree from Columbia in Middle Eastern languages and cultures. Harris has contributed translations of the classical Sufi writer al-Qushayri. She is involved in peace and justice movements and lectures on progressive Islam.

In her chapter published in Gisela Webb's anthology of articles by American Muslim women, *Windows of Faith* (2000), Harris makes the following critique (p. 174):

> Islam is supposed to be the religion of truth. At least, it is in
> the Qur'an. It was in the words and actions of the Prophet.
> Is it, in the lives of Muslims today? Why does 'Islamic
> reality' so often seem like a smaller, poorer, and more
> uncomfortable space to occupy than 'regular reality'? Why
> is the 'islamization of knowledge' a project going nowhere?
> Why are so many believers so defensive, so offensive, about
> their faith?

This quote illustrates the activism espoused by some American Sufi
women who are willing to criticise authoritarian structures and
attitudes.

Lex Hixon, also a Helveti, was sensitive to gender issues as well,
but somewhat more conservative, at least in his formal comments
featured in the collection *American Jihad: Islam After Malcolm X*
(1994: p. 197).

> The Prophet, upon him be peace, was extremely sensitive to
> women. He had nine wives, whom he adored and whom he
> attended to with more care and attention than the normal
> husband gives to one wife. And so that we feel that follow-
> ing his way, the love and courtesy of men to women, is
> something very essential in Islam. We don't defend various
> cultural patterns that have sprung up in so-called Islamic
> countries which might be seen to be oppressive of women.
> But we hold basic equality of men and women.

He also states (p. 197):

> In Mexico we have a woman who leads our zikr and who's
> the head of the community there. She has the permission
> from the grand sheik in Istanbul to do this. She doesn't lead
> the prayers. A man leads the prayers in Islam because that's
> the Sunnah. That was the way the Holy Prophet, upon
> whom be peace, did it. So we like to preserve those beautiful
> ancient ways of behaving.

Here we see Hixon negotiating between *sharia* compliance and providing leadership opportunities for Sufi women.

An article by Gwendolyn Zohara Simmons in Webb's anthology *Windows of Faith* identifies her as 'a Sunni Muslim and a member of the Sheikh Muhammad Raheem Bawa Muhaiyaddeen Mosque and fellowship in Philadelphia'. Simmons, an African American, directly confronts the oppression of women in some Muslim contexts, including the United States, in the light of her personal experiences in the American civil rights movement (p. 203):

> Therefore, my relationship with my chosen religion, Islam, has been fraught with ambivalence and tension. My biggest problem has been with the traditional depiction of women and our role in both the religion and in society. You may ask how I came to be a Muslim given the above brief biographical account and given the stereotypical depiction in the West of Islam as the most misogynist of the three Abrahamic traditions.
>
> My conversion to Sunni Islam was through the example and guidance of a Sufi teacher from Sri Lanka, Sheikh Muhammad Raheem Bawa Muhaiyuddeen. I was drawn to the religion by its mystical and spiritual aspects as taught by him. The beautiful prayer rituals, the month of fasting, the pilgrimage to Mecca.

According to Simmons, the Sufi master Guru Bawa in his teaching supported women as manifesting the feminine qualities of Allah while giving them practical recognition in participation and leadership. His was a twentieth-century Islam that adhered to the foundations and to the eternal and universal principles of the religion while it embraced the knowledge and understanding of this era.

Another remarkable work relevant to the theme of gender and American Sufism is the autobiographical study of two women from Los Angeles who grew up in the 1950s. The author of *Finding Fran* (1998), Lois Banner, is a professor of women's history at the University of Southern California, while her friend, Noura Durkee (Fran), was a participant in many spiritual movements and eventually converted to Islam through Sufism. Banner asks why their lives took such different paths, hers to feminism and Fran's to Islam? Beyond exploring cultural trends and historical timing, Banner displays her sympathies with Fran's Muslim perspective and relates it to her own feminist awakening.

This book traces the currents operating in the life of Noura Durkee, prominent in such American Sufi movements as the Lama Foundation and the Islamic village at Abiquiu, New Mexico. Travel is a significant element of spiritual experience for Fran and other American Sufis, from her participation in the Pir Vilayat Sufi camps at Chamonix of the 1970s on to Jerusalem, then Mecca, Cairo and finally back to the United States. In Banner's tracing of some of the eclectic spiritual currents running through Fran/Noura's experience one finds: Gurdjieff groups, Pir Vilayat Khan's Sufi Order, the Lama Foundation (a Sufi-influenced spiritual centre in New Mexico), Baba Ram Das (a Harvard professor turned Yogic guru) and Shadhili Sufism. As an interesting twist, the feminist academic Banner confesses in the introduction her own involvement in universal Sufism through the Dances of Universal Peace and her taking initiation in the Sufi order of Pir Vilayat Khan. The tone of the book is set by Banner trying to appreciate Fran's path as an authentic American woman's search for spirituality. The conclusion is that smart, competent people, including American females, might find something valuable in embracing Islamic Sufism.

An incident illustrating American female Sufis rebelling or 'acting up' is one that I personally witnessed at an International Association of Sufism Conference in the Bay Area. A Rifa'i sheikh from Kuwait was leading a collective *dhikr*, in which a succession of universalist and *sharia*-oriented teachers took turns in directing the likewise mixed audience in Islamic chants. The sheikh commented that since some female participants were not covering their hair during the practices, the angels could not be present at the gathering. Some American women were outraged and protested by walking out, in a few cases provocatively tossing their heads as if shaking their cascading tresses in defiance.

In brief summary, it is clear that female members of Western Sufi movements take positions about gender along some sort of continuum from subversion and activism directed towards challenging and reforming traditional Muslim practices to acceptance of the rationale for 'gender complementarity'. The concept that maleness and femaleness function as distinct energies is expressed not only by *sharia*-oriented movements such as the Naqshbandi-Haqqanis, but also in certain teachings of the universalist Sufi Islamia Ruhaniat Society and the Sufi order, where specific movements, dances or practices are cultivated as part of attuning to essentially different gender frequencies.

Conclusions

In summary, 'American' aspects of Sufi movements in the United States indicate that this is one manifestation of Islam that quickly adapts to the local cultural context. 'American' Sufis are noteworthy for their inroads into popular culture, for example in the realms of publishing and music. In the case of perennialist or universal Sufi groups, their identification with Islamic spirituality allows their integration into New Age and religious healing circles. Certain Sufis of the past, for example, Rumi and Ibn Arabi, are particularly amenable to this cross-over reading.

Probably the most significant impacts of American Sufi movements on 'mainstream' Islamic discourse and organisations in America occur through the lectures and Internet writings of *sharia*-oriented Sufis who minimise their identification with specific sheikhs and *tariqas* and recover acceptable terminology and interpretations of Islamic spiritual understandings.

Yet another development occurring among American Sufis who are in greater interaction with mainstream youth movements and institutions is the advocacy of indigenisation that would draw on indigenous aspects of American religion: for example, the appreciation of and response to the natural beauty of the United States, in some cases through an affinity with Native American traditions. For example, Schuon's group had an interest in Native American ritual, and one group of American Muslim converts called their annual gatherings an 'American Muslim Powwow'. Yet another attempt to fuse Islam and American religious aesthetics arises in the suggestion that mosques should be constructed in a style like that used by the quietist American movement, the Shakers, who are noted for their dignity and simplicity, rather than attempting to copy Middle Eastern architectural forms. In response to the Islamic monoculture promulgated by internationalist movements, some American Sufis have advocated the development of a distinctive American Muslim style of dress. I also note that progressive Muslim discussion lists have a high proportion of Euro-American converts and American Sufi participants, demonstrating the popularity of this interpretation of Islam among such groups.

4

SUFISM IN RUSSIA
Nostalgia for Revelation

Ravil Bukharaev

In his books on Islam in Russia, Alexandre Bennigsen says that Sufism, which he describes as 'parallel Islam', seemingly disappeared among the Muslims of the European part of Russia after 1924. Another famous scholar, Hamid Algar, states, however, that the five-centuries-old tradition could not have totally disappeared within the seventy-year period of Soviet rule. He refers to a number of Soviet publications on the history of Sufism in Russia as showing that the issue of Sufism within mainstream Russian Islam still retains its relevance.

However, the history of Sufism in Russia is still very patchy and remains, in large part, very much a matter of circumstantial speculation. Recently, Tatar and Bashkir researchers of Sufism in the Volga–Urals area have tried to bring into their field of study the books compiled and written by two well-known Islamic scholars of the beginning of the twentieth century. Those books are *Asar*, a biographical reference book in several volumes by Riza Fahretdinov (1859–1936), and *Talfik al-Ahbar wa Talkih al-Asar fi Wakaig Kazan wa Bulgar wa al-Muluk at-Tatar* (The combinative work on the history of Kazan, Bulgar and the Tatar kings) written by Sheikh Murad Ramzi (1853–1936) and published in Orenburg in 1908. Both scholars were, it is claimed, Sufi followers of the 'last great sheikh' of the Volga–Urals region, Zainullah Rasulev (1835–1917), who was the most prominent Sufi teacher in Russia of the nineteenth and twentieth centuries. In the last mentioned book, inspired by and written under the supervision of Sheikh Rasulev, Murad Ramzi also narrates the history of Sufism in Russia and brings forward many names and genealogies of Sufi teachers. At the same time these works, like many others compiled in the nineteenth and twentieth centuries, require caution as to their claims and the reliability of their historical data.

The sad lack of reliable sources is the main reason for historical ambiguity in respect of Islam and Sufism in Russia, which results from the fact that, after the Russian conquest of the Kazan Khanate in 1552, the critical Muslim historiography of the Volga–Urals region all but ceased to exist. Another reason for a weaker understanding of the Volga–Urals Sufi history in the last century or so, as opposed, for instance, to the Sufi history of the Russian North Caucasus, is that it had much less political relevance in the eyes of Russian and Western researchers.

However, the issue of Sufism is indeed being revived in Russia following the recent growth of political and militant trends in Russian Islam at large. In attempts to 'rein in' the present uncontrollable developments in Islamic thought, which for the last ten years has experienced the various 'unwelcome' influences of Arab and Pakistani visions of 'politicised Islam', be it the image of an Islamic state by Mawlana Mawdudi, or the Wahhabi 'purification' of customary Islamic ways, the Russian *ulama* (religious scholars) in their historical partnership with the Russian authorities are trying to lure Russian Muslims back into what they call 'the traditional, peace-loving and tolerant' Islam of 'the forefathers'.

Today, this vision of traditional Islam seems to include the Sufi tradition as well. In April 2000, the Muslim Spiritual Board of the Republic of Tatarstan organised a conference called 'The Tatar Sufi Traditions'. The analytical paper prepared for this conference, which remains unpublished in the board's archive, says the following:

> The analysis of the present situation in Tatar Islam shows that various forces are trying to occupy the empty 'Sufi niche' in the socio-religious awareness of the Tatars. Their activity proves that the problem is ripe for resolution. Sufism will re-appear in any case, and it is clear that it cannot be left without control.

After mentioning the present-day activities of the Turkish 'Sufi brotherhoods' even in the Tatar state educational system, the paper goes on to suggest that there has evolved a great need to spread the tradition of the Naqshbandi order among Russian Muslims, which could 'make it easier to fight back against the Wahhabi and other extreme visions of Islam'. Moreover, the same paper calls for the taking over of the practices of political life of Uzbekistan, where this order apparently 'plays a positive role in assuring the loyalty of the Muslims to the present political authority'. The last statement is all the more illustrative of the intentions of the bitterly disunited Russian official *ulama* for those who know the realities of Uzbek religious life, with its apprehension and intolerance of the political establishment towards any independent religious thinking. Considering the very nature of Sufism as a historical transition of *the thirst for ever-living Revelation* through the chain of spiritual teachers and the partly secretive nature of this process, the attempts to kick-start the network of Sufi activities in Russia out of purely political motives seem to reveal a measure of confusion on the part of the Russian *ulama* in their efforts to understand the roots of the religious processes of today.

The Sufi way of knowing God is distinguished from other Muslim ways of acquiring information about the world and its Creator by its concentration on a person's own ability to perceive Him without help from the outside world, except from the teacher (*murshid*). However, it is difficult to single out 'a pure Sufi' in the first centuries of Sufism. In any case, as the history of Sufism in Volga Bulgaria, and much later Russia, shows, the most prominent Sufis of that area never practised 'pure' or ascetic Sufism, but always combined it with science and religious duties.

In the light of the above, this author views Sufism as an inherited yearning for a wider and deeper perception of the Revelation, and Sufis as the bearers of this yearning. They are also the predecessors of the much wider rethinking of the Revelation, when the cycle of history turned and the 'doors of independent thinking', or *ijtihad*, became open for ever growing numbers of Muslims, as happened on the threshold of the twentieth century. I argue that Sufism, as it was, virtually ceased to exist in Russia, not because of the Communist persecution, but because all its yearning and creative energy found their way into the broad revivalist movement of Jadidism as the process of Islamic renewal and overall revitalisation of Islamic thought.

Thus the historic role of the Sufis was to keep the thirst for the coming Revelation alive, and it is in this sense that I call Sufism a 'nostalgia for Revelation' at a time when all other doors of actual rethinking of the Revelation and its relations to the world were 'closed' by the consensus of traditionalists. Once these 'doors of *ijtihad*' are opened, the closeness to God as the purpose of life may be obtained by a Muslim through many educational avenues, without special skills and mechanisms devised by Sufi practices, because then the idea of the living God and the possibility of approaching Him through deeper delving into the message of Revelation becomes available to many, and not only to closed Sufi circles.

The movement of Jadidism in Russia is proof enough that, on the threshold of the revival of widespread independent Islamic thinking, authentic Sufi teachings find their place in a much wider picture of Islamic revival. It seems especially true for Russia, where all major Sufi figures eventually played their role in the Jadidist revitalisation and the spread of Islam far beyond the borders of Russia – as far as Japan and northern China.

Historical perspective

We now turn to the issue of Sufism and to the role of the Sufis in Russian Muslim history. This history, at least according to the surviving records of Muslim historians and geographers, began in the middle of the ninth century, when some outposts of Central Asian Islam took root on the banks of the Volga and the Kama rivers, in Volga Bulgaria. With the establishment of the Khazar empire, which in the ninth century took a firm hold of the Volga waterway, the northern trade with the Muslim south went down the left bank of the Volga to Khawarism, where it traditionally joined the Great Silk Route to the East and to the West, but also went further south to the domains of the Arab Caliphate. The booming trade based on the fact that Bulgar goods were not available elsewhere, along with the political necessity of securing it in the hands of the Volga Bulgaria merchants and nobles who controlled the Kama–Urals waterway, precipitated closer ties with Islamic Central Asia. The acceptance of Islam by the state of Volga Bulgaria, which happened in 922, took place over the heads of Central Asian rulers and *ulama*, directly from the seat of the Baghdadi caliph, apparently in order to show the strength and independence of the Volga Bulgaria vis-à-vis its economic and political partners in Central Asia. The wealth of knowledge of Islam and its sciences always came to the Volga–Urals area from and through Central Asia, and this tradition, despite all the trials and tribulations of history, persisted over one thousand years until the middle of the nineteenth century. The currents of information coming into the domain of Volga–Urals Islam were obviously bringing with them not only practical, but also spiritual knowledge, above and beyond traditional rules and practices.

We may make educated guesses of when and how the notion of Sufism first came into the geographical area of our interest. Using circumstantial evidence and assuming that the ways and channels of information did not change too much in the course of the tenth and eleventh centuries, we may deduce that the traditions of earlier Sufis were to some extent known on the Volga–Kama crossroads as well. Indeed, the execution of Mansur al-Hallaj took place in exactly the same year as the acceptance of Islam by the Volga Bulgaria kingdom at the hands of Khalif al-Muktadir's ambassador, i.e. in 922. The story of al-Hallaj and his relationship with traditionalist *ulama* was still fresh for the founder of Central Asian Sufism, Ahmed Yassavi, in the twelfth century and greatly inspired his poems.

The twelfth century in the history of Volga Bulgaria was a time of relative peace and prosperity, and Sufism rarely made itself visible in such periods of civil calm. We may only guess whether the culture of Sufi convents or *khanakas* penetrated Volga Bulgaria and its environs as early as the tenth to the twelfth centuries. Thus, for lack of written historical data, we cannot research the beginnings of Sufism on the banks of the Volga and the Kama with any degree of certainty. At the same time, we know of a number of Islamic scholars from Volga Bulgaria who lived and worked in Central Asia, Iran and Magrib, where they were certainly aware of the Sufi teachings of their time and may well have been among the students of famous Sufis.

Having subdued the rebellious people whose name is recorded in Chinese sources as Ta-Ta, the victorious Mongolian ruler Chingiz Khan (1162–1227) turned his eye to China and the Muslim civilisations of the West. Of the latter, Khwarism became the first victim of Chingiz Khan's desire for world domination. Having conquered the main cities of Central Asia such as Bukhara, Samarkand, Urgench and Merv, the Mongol armies launched an attack on the Kipchak Steppe, where in 1223 they defeated the combined armies of the local Turks and the Russians. In the autumn of the same year the Mongol general, Subedey, attempted to take Volga Bulgaria. This failed, as did two further attempts in 1229 and 1232, when the Mongols were repelled by the staunch resistance of the Bulgars and the Russians. But this was the last military success of Volga Bulgaria. In the autumn of 1236 the Mongols captured the city of Bolgar and reduced most of the neighbouring towns to ashes. The last sovereign of independent Volga Bulgaria, Ilham Khan, who had successfully organised the resistance of 1223 and 1229, was killed in the final battle with his formidable enemy.

With the demolition of orthodox Muslim institutions and hierarchy by the Mongols in the early thirteenth century, the role of the Sufis in Volga Bulgaria greatly increased, as indeed was the case in all the Muslim land conquered and destroyed by the Mongols. The wandering dervishes became the main bearers of the message of Islam not only in Volga Bulgaria, but all over the Great Steppe, Dasht-I-Kypchak. Their influence was such that even the rulers of the Golden Horde became Muslims through their efforts, which once again changed the fate of Islam in the area of our interest. The Mongol nobility, who at first despised 'those decadent Muslims' for their urban rather than nomadic way of life, soon began to live in towns. From the newly built city of Sarai on the lower Volga to Kazan a chain of towns of varying sizes came into existence, and under the rule of the Golden Horde khan, Berke (1257–66), Islam became the official religion. The local form of Turkish became the accepted state language and was written in Arabic characters. Literature once more began to flourish, the greatest influences being, as they were elsewhere, the Sufi works of Rumi, Sadi, Hafiz and others. The Tatar historian Shigabutdin Mardzhani (d. 1889), in his treatise *Wafiyyat al-Aslaf wa Tahiyyat al-Ahlaf*, describes one of the presumably many Sufi personages of this age, naming him as Hasan Bulgari, follower of the Khurasani Sheikh Saatdin al Khamawi, who had to escape to Central Asia from Bolgar after being, most probably, accused of heresy. And yet this age was still favourable to Sufis because of the nomadic tolerance of the Mongolian rulers, who also accepted Islam from the hands of wandering dervishes and did not look too much into the theological differences between the orthodox traditionalists and the Sufi seekers after truth, whose ways often deviated from the dogmatic preferences of the orthodox leaders of the age.

The Mongol capital, Sarai, which was described by the Arab geographer Ibn Battuta as 'one of the most beautiful cities, full of people, with beautiful bazaars and wide avenues', was also the home of many Sufi poets, most of whom are known to us only by their names. One of the earliest pieces of verse which has come down to us from this period is the fairly lengthy poem *Jamjama Sultan* (The Skull King) by Hisam Kyatib. Several manuscripts of the work are extant and recent research by Tatar scholars has shown that it was completed around 1368–9 in one of the Volga towns. The author's pen-name Kyatib, 'scribe', probably refers to his profession as a scribe of one of the civic or religious institutions. The story of the poem is a reworking of the old legend of the skull, which once belonged to a proud monarch. This gives the poet plenty of scope to reflect upon the follies of humankind and the fate awaiting humans in the life hereafter. A similar theme is taken up by the author of the famous *Kisek-bash* (Severed Head), which also belongs to the Golden Horde period.

One of the most outstanding poets of this period was Saif-i Sarai (1321–96), whose verse is contained in two manuscripts now in Leiden. From the pen-name he assumed it is obvious that he had strong links with the capital, Sarai, which at this time was ruled by Uzbek Khan. Research has shown that he was born in the town of Kamyshly, which can probably be identified as modern Kamyshin in the Volgograd region of Russia. To escape the plague and civil disorder, which marked the general decline of the Golden Horde, Saif-i Sarai fled to Egypt, where according to his own writings he stayed from 1380 to 1395. A number of Golden Horde scholars of logic and jurisprudence were already established in Cairo, and as an outstanding man of letters Saif-i Sarai was welcomed in their midst. While in Cairo he wrote a Turkish version of the *Gulistan* (The Rose-Garden) by the famous Persian poet, Sheikh Sadi. He dedicated his work, which was entitled *Gulistan bit-Turki*, to his patron, the Emir Taikhas. Saif-i Sarai died in Cairo in 1396, and with his death the literary and cultural ambience of the Golden Horde period came to an end. The once united country split into a number of separate khanates, among them that of Kazan, from which time another chapter opens in the history of the Volga Tatars and their Sufi poetry.

Again, little is known of the life of the poet Muhammadyar, whose major surviving works, *Tuhfaye Mardan* (The Gift to Young Men, 1539), and *Nuri Sodur* (The Light of Hearts, 1542), have much in common with the poems ascribed to Hoja Ahmed Yassavi, and are greatly influenced by Naqshbandi teachings, which through ties with Central Asia and Persia had become widespread in Volga Bulgaria and the Kazan Khanate. Both works concern ethical and moral issues and are divided into several chapters, each dealing with a particular virtue such as justice, patience or generosity. Like other Sufis, Muhammadyar apparently preferred an independent existence away from the comfort and intrigues of the court. He stands out as one of the foremost poets of the Kazan Khanate.

The annexation of the Kazan Khanate by Ivan the Terrible in 1552 was in many ways more terrible and destructive than the attack of Timur Tamerlane a century and a half earlier. Not only were the Tatars under foreign domination, but they were forbidden from entering their own cities under pain of death. The survivors were ordered to settle thirty miles away from any large town, and for that reason their traditional culture was effectively banished to the countryside. From that time onwards all major poets were born and educated in the villages, which themselves became seats of learning. Since Islam had become a persecuted faith, from the late sixteenth century well into the eighteenth such activities had to be carried on in a clandestine fashion. Mosques were destroyed and Orthodox Christian churches were built on the same site. After several decades, when trade in Kazan had declined, the Tatars were allowed to reside on the outskirts of their former illustrious capital in the Old and New Tatar settlements, which now form a part of the city of Kazan.

The fate of the last poet of the Kazan Khanate, Mevla Koly, is in many ways indicative of what was happening to Tatar religious life throughout the seventeenth century. His real name was Bairamgali Koliev, and because of his mystic background he was popularly known as Bimka Sufi. Mevla Koly's poems strongly reflect Sufi traditions dating back to the age of Ahmed Yassavi, at the same time displaying and making use of local motifs and images which can be found in the verse of Kol Gali and earlier folk songs. He, like many Turkish poets, calls his poems *hikmet*, from the Arabic word for 'wisdom' (*hikma*). The *hikmet,* a Turkish quatrain of seven or eleven syllables usually composed on the subject of the miracles of the Prophet, with pronouncements on the vanity of the world and the virtues of the ascetic life, go back to the age of Ahmed Yassavi. In the *divan* dedicated to his teacher, Mullah Mamai, Mevla Koly writes:

> Dear friends! This *hikmet* was written
> In the year 1088 after the Hijra,
> In the region near the city of Bolgar
> By the sinner and tormentor, Maula Koly.

Until the mid-eighteenth century, the Russian Muslims had no official leadership and the maintenance and development of Islam was largely in the hands of Sufi teachers like Mevla Koly himself. However, for all the wealth of poetry that Sufism bequeathed to Russian Islam, the history of Sufism in Russia up to the eighteenth century can only be called patchy, especially where the chain of *silsila*, or hereditary Sufi teachings and practices, is concerned.

It is all the more difficult to see the real historical scheme of the role and function of the Sufis in what became Russia after the conquest of Kazan by Ivan the Terrible, in that there is a lack of real historic data, and many legends and wishful thinking have crept into the historiography of Russian Islam. It is this false or imagined history that is being widely used in Russia, especially today, when the need for historical awareness among the Muslim nation of Russia has speeded up the writing of historical books and articles serving mostly political rather than scholarly purposes. Earlier books of history, especially the famous work by M. Khudyakov on the history of the Kazan Khanate, are used without any critical approach, even when some of the material contained in them was dismissed as early as the nineteenth century.

One thing is certain when we speak about the role of the Sufis in Russia, and that is their task as religious educators and preachers of Islam in a situation where no legal educational system existed due to political calamities or outright religious persecution. Therefore, to speak of Sufism in the Kazan Khanate or its remnants in the seventeenth century, we have to turn our attention to the systems of Islamic religious education that were in existence in Russia from the sixteenth century to the middle of the eighteenth.

We know about the existence of the main *madrasa* (religious school) of Kazan, which was situated at the Dzhami mosque of Kol Sharif. The fervour with which the students of this *madrasa* along with their teacher defended Kazan against the Russian onslaught of 1552 points to the fact that it was as much a Sufi institution with its staunch *murshid–murid* (teacher–student) relationship, as a so-called orthodox religious school. The later history of Russian *madrasas* shows the same pattern of being not only a general religious school but also, as a rule, a Sufi circle with a Sufi leader called an ishan as its head and master (ishan was a Central Asian and later Russian synonym for a sheikh or Sufi leader). If this is true, then the notion of a certain antagonism between 'the free-thinking' Sufis and dogmatic and traditionalist *ulama* in the Kazan Khanate will have to be viewed afresh.

In this sense, the picture of Sufism in which many members of the 'orthodox' *ulama* were at the same time Sufi ishans is as peculiar to the history of Russian Islam as its two hundred years of all but underground existence after the fall of Kazan. Being and staying a Muslim of whatever ideology was apparently far more important in times of troubles than any arguments of a religious nature. Tolerance towards the Sufis as an intellectual class of their own was all the more understandable in that it is to them that Islam in Russia, first and foremost, owes its extent and growth. This role of Sufi dervish preachers cannot be overestimated even in the age of the Kazan Khanate, for their efforts in converting the non-Muslim population to Islam was as persistent as it was continuous. Not only would the wandering dervish contribute to widening the Russian *umma* or Muslim congregation. The Sufi institutions, whether it was a circle of followers of a particular ishan around the saintly tombs, or a village school run by a certain Sufi master, were also centres of missionary activity, both in 'commending Islam to non-Muslims and in helping the newly converted to take it to their hearts'. It seems that such Sufi centres were particularly dynamic in the regions where official religious authority was less prominent, that is to say in the Vyatka–Urals region and the districts located between the Kazan and Kasymov khanates: the spread and strengthening of Islamic beliefs among the Mishar and Karinsk Tatars, especially the former, offer enough evidence for this supposition, as the Mishars often inhabited areas outside the direct control either of the Kazan or the Kasymov khanates. The Sufi schools were therefore tolerated, if not permitted, as educational and missionary centres, although official religious authority never reconciled itself, whatever compromises were made, to the existence of centres of religious authority outside their control. Nevertheless, a particular Sufi *tariqa*, that is, Naqshbandiyya, was always renowned in Russian Islam for its political correctness and humble restraint vis-à-vis the official *ulama*, so much so that the members of this group of religious leaders, as we have already stated, were frequently sympathisers, if not followers, of Naqshbandiyya thought.

As elsewhere in the Islamic world of the time, certain Sufi practices slowly came to be recognised in the area of our interest as part of traditional Islam: this is true, for instance, in regard of the religious festival of celebrating the Prophet's birthday, which originated in its present form not earlier than the 1420s and came to be an essential part of popular Muslim beliefs and practices later on. Despite all possible arguments between the official *ulama* and the Naqshbandiyya Sufis, the existence of the Sufi schools and missionary centres proved crucial for the very existence of Islamic culture after the Russian conquest of the Kazan Khanate.

After the fall of Kazan, when the whole business of safeguarding Islam effectively passed into the hands of village mullahs and other knowledgeable persons called, in Tatar, *abyzes* (derived from Arabic *hafiz*, or one knowing the Quran by heart), there is a definite gap in our understanding of how and through what medium the knowledge and, more importantly, the practice of Sufism was passed from one Sufi teacher to another. Maula Koly seems to present the only example of a wandering teacher and Sufi poet who at the same time fulfilled the duties of a community leader, or *abyz*.

As in the years after the Mongol onslaught, the Sufis in what became Russia after the fall of Kazan and Astrakhan in the sixteenth century became the only significant religious force, which helped to keep the faith alive. It was all the more difficult, in that in the Russian Codex of 1649 the preaching of Islam to non-Muslims became punishable by being burnt at the stake. As the population of the erstwhile Muslim lands became increasingly mixed ethnically, such preaching had become all but impossible and had to be cautiously secretive. Here, the ways of Sufism became the only ways of propagating the faith, and the authority of the Sufi teachers of the time was safeguarded in the popular memory, even if in a very sketchy way.

In the sixteenth and seventeenth centuries, economic and spiritual connections with Central Asia, which played a major role in the spreading of Sufi ideas, were severely damaged due to the disturbances caused, first of all, by Russian wars against the Kazan, Astrakhan and Siberian khanates; second, by wars between Turkey and Iran; and, third, by the Time of Troubles in Russia. Under such circumstances, the now Russian Muslims were reduced to sheer survival, as even their livelihood was under constant threat from the Russian authorities. The policy of forced baptism was in full swing for a whole century and a half after the fall of Kazan, and even in 1713 an ordinance of Peter the Great compelled the Muslims to receive baptism under threat of economic deprivation. The history of anti-Islamic persecution in Russia from the fifteenth through to the seventeenth century is well recorded, and the very survival of Islam in such conditions represents a miracle of history.

We may even say that in view of the lack of Islamic infrastructure like mosques, *madrasas* and an established spiritual hierarchy, the entire body of Islam in Russia became, in the seventeenth century, a Sufi Islam, using for its survival as a faith the Sufi literary heritage and Sufi traditions of safeguarding the graves of saints, for even the sanctity of cemeteries was often denied to the Muslims of Russia. Thus the tradition of a special reverence for cemeteries, in each of which there was, or was guessed to be, the tomb of a saint, was further strengthened in the seventeenth century by the fact that Muslim cemeteries were simply being destroyed. One of the most striking examples of this is the Church of the Resurrection among the ruins of the medieval city of Bolgar, in the foundations of which lay the gravestones from Muslim cemeteries. No wonder, then, that the sanctity and respect for Islamic graveyards started to play such a prominent role, not only in the everyday life of Russian Muslims, but also in the historical writings of Kazan Tatar historians like S. Mardzhani and Qayyum Nasiri. Almost every village described in their writings could boast the grave of a saint and, knowing the state of affairs in Russia in the seventeenth and eighteenth centuries, such saints could and would be Sufis.

However, except surviving examples of Sufi poetry, all that could be said about the state of Sufism in the seventeenth-century Russia once again amounts to circumstantial evidence and educated guess-work. Yet about Sufis of the eighteenth and nineteenth centuries we know much more, thanks to the selfless and scrupulous work by Shigabutdin Mardzhani, who can in all fairness be called the father of the Tatar historiography of today. In his book *Personalities and Memorable Events* (first published in 1897), he gives us many clues, from which we can construe the main trends of the development of Sufism in Russia. Most importantly, from the works of Mardzhani and later Tatar historical records, we see that eighteenth-century Sufism on the banks of the Volga and the Kama rivers had four main sources, namely,

1   the Sufi heritage of the Kazan Khanate (1552 to the beginning of the eighteenth century);
2   the Sufi heritage of Bukhara and Kabul (the eighteenth to the middle of the nineteenth century);
3   the Sufi heritage of Daghestan (the eighteenth to the middle of the nineteenth century);
4   the Sufi heritage of Turkey (from the middle of the nineteenth century until the 1920s).

As for the Sufi heritage of the Kazan Khanate, we can only say that it existed among the Sufis of Russia as the sense of their belonging to the ancestral Islam of Volga Bulgaria and the Kazan Khanate. For all feeling of Islamic unity, the sense of belonging to the northern Turkic domain of Islam, with its Yassavi-Naqshbandi Sufi legacy, was and is very strong among the Muslims of European Russia and Siberia. However, this peculiar sense of belonging to the Volga Bulgaria Sufi chain very seldom came to the surface in Russian Muslim history, but once revealed itself in a most rebellious way in the otherwise very law-abiding Russian *umma* of the nineteenth century.

In this respect, the appearance in the Kazan district in the nineteenth century of the Ishan Bahavetdin Vaisov movement is an interesting phenomenon, pointing to the existence of the peculiar undercurrents of Russian Sufism, which now and then resurface even today, although more in political than religious disguise. The very idea, which made Vaisov famous and contributed to his destruction, was not a new one. In the 1760s, a personage called Mullah Murad was already preaching the necessity to restore the Volga Bulgar state and to safeguard all religious traditions, which, as he believed, came from the Volga Bulgaria age. But if the time of Mullah Murad was one of the persecution of the faith and many peasant uprisings, in which Tatar and Bashkir Muslims took a very active part, the founder of the Vaisov movement lived and preached in very different circumstances.

Bahavetdin Khamzin-Vaisov, the founder of the pro-Bolgar 'Firkai Nadzhiya' (Regiment of God) movement, was born in 1804 in the village of Molvino, or, in Tatar, Mulla Ile, in the now Zelenodosk district of the Republic of Tatarstan. Known to his followers and admirers, both past and present, as a popular leader, a Sufi philosopher and a poet who later sent his poems in letters to many officials starting with the Tsar and Tsarina of Russia and ending with the attorneys and district judges of the Kazan district, he first studied in Kazan and then went on a journey to Turkestan and Bukhara, which suggests his closeness to the Yassavi legacy as well as his acquaintance with the Sufi teachers of Bukhara. Later he founded a 'Muslim Academy' in Kazan, a centre totally separate from all other Islamic institutions in Russia, which comprised a mosque and *madrasa*, as well as the headquarters – the so-called Spiritual Board – of his movement of civil disobedience to the Russian authorities extending as far as to the introduction of passports issued by the Board. The members of this movement stood not only against the 'un-Islamic' governments of Russia, but also against their fellow Muslims, inasmuch as they considered themselves the true progeny of the Volga Bulgars as opposed to the Tatars, the very appellation of which they deemed insulting. The Vaisov movement called itself a Naqhsbandiyya movement, but, as opposed to the usually quiet and meditative ways of other followers of Naqshbandiyya in European Russia, they proved to be so militant and so loyal to their leader both in word and deed that the *murids* of Vaisov were not only prepared to pay for their ishan with their lives, but actually did so. In the 1880s the Vaisov movement was at the core of several peasant uprisings in the Kazan district, and that became the last straw in the uneasy relationship of the movement with both Russian authorities and Kazan Tatar Muslims. In 1884 the headquarters of Vaisov's 'Regiment of God' were stormed for seven days, and the leader was arrested and put in an asylum, where he died in 1893.

The Vaisov movement did not, however, die along with its founder. The son of Bahavetdin Vaisov, Gainan, survived a range of persecutions, being sent as an exile to Siberia in 1894, and to Sahalin in 1895, but he returned to Kazan in 1906 after the first Russian Revolution. In the new conditions he managed to revive the structure of the movement and became an Islamic revolutionary, still pressing for the freedom from un-Islamic laws and regulations. The Vaisov movement interested Leo Tolstoy and the writer met Gainan Vaisov in 1909. It seems that Vaisov's political radicalism frightened the great writer, who was interested mainly in the Islamic views of the Kazan Sufi leader. Later, the political zeal of Gainan Vaisov led him into the camp of the Bolsheviks, and he died in 1918 fighting the Tatar uprising in Kazan.

When the present-day Muslim *ulama* of Russia think of resurrecting the traditions of Sufism, they should first of all take heed of the Vaisov movement, in which radical nationalist tendencies were firmly entwined with the somewhat superficial Sufi ideology. If the Russian *ulama* assume that they can always control the so-called Sufi developments in Russia, the historical example of the regular militancy of the Vaisov movement, as well as the political legacy of Ishan Kurbangaliev, of whom we shall speak further, should make anyone think twice about the invariably 'positive role' of Sufism 'in assuring the loyalty of Muslims to the present political authority'.

However, long before the excesses of the Vaisov movement and the unrelenting struggle of the *murids* of Ishan Kurbangaliev against the Red Army in the civil war of 1918–20, the legacy of Volga Bulgaria Sufism, which makes itself so visible in the poetry of Mukhammedyar and Maula Koly, was carried on and, in a way, developed by another prominent Sufi, of whom Mardzhani writes in his book. This was one Murtaza bin Kotlygysh who died in 1723, leaving a number of disciples, whose descendants were known to affirm their belonging to his *silsilah* (chain of Sufi teachers) by saying: 'We are from the progeny of Hoja Ahmad Yassavi.' Looking at the personality of Murtaza bin Kotlygysh, we may suggest that it is he and the likes of him who filled the gap in the Sufi chains, which originated in the Kazan Khanate and were carried on by person- alities similar to Maula Koly. It is interesting that it is in the time of Murtaza bin Kotlygysh that the Sufi connection to the area of our interest and Central Asia was established afresh and started to run parallel to the Sufi legacy of the Kazan Khanate, sometimes replacing it altogether.

One of the *murids* of Murtaza bin Kotlygysh, Mansur Burunduki, was, according to Mardzhani, the first Russian Muslim who went to Bukhara for additional Sufi education and, upon returning, became a bitter enemy of his teacher. Mardzhani even says that Mansur Burunduki killed one of his own followers, when the latter dared to marry a girl the teacher had an eye on himself. To escape punish- ment, says Mardzhani, the murderer accepted Christianity and thus avoided being put in jail. This historical anecdote is nevertheless very characteristic of its own time, because it tells us not only of the existence of at least two different visions and chains of Sufism at the beginning of the eighteenth century in Russia, but also places the Sufi arguments against the background of religious coercion by the Russian authorities, when even a criminal Muslim had a hope of escaping punishment by simply accepting Christianity.

One other Sufi personality who was among the first to visit Bukhara and receive initiation was Gabdelkarim Kargaly of the village of Kargala near Orenburg. Mardzhani writes that he received permission to practise Sufism and have followers from a certain

'Zhakriah' order, whose adepts apparently practised the loud *dhikr* (commemoration), which was very seldom, if at all, practised among the Russian Naqshbandiyya. However, the tradition of going to Bukhara and Kabul for initiation became well established and continued for about a century. Interestingly, the Tatar ishans, who studied Sufism in Central Asia and Afghanistan, brought with them a written permission in the form of a blessing from their teacher. So, in the eighteenth century, Sufism in Russia became somewhat bureaucratic, as without such written permission the skills and knowledge of a Sufi leader were not recognised by his fellows and contemporaries.

Among the Sufi teachers of the eighteenth to the beginning of the nineteenth century named by Mardzhani in his book, the two most prominent are: Ishan-Khalifa Niyaz Koly Turkmani, who was also the chief imam of the central mosque of Bukhara, and Ishan Faez Khan bin Hozur Khan Kabuli. Among the *murids* of the first of them, who, in their turn, had followers in the Middle Volga area, were Fazyl Kizlyavi (d. 1812) and Davlet Shah Maskavi (d. 1831). However, among the most famous students of the Bukharan Ishan Niyaz Koly was the reformer of Tatar Islam, the scholar and spiritual fighter in the name of Islam, Gabdennasyr Kursavi, a personality who can be called 'the Tatar al-Hallaj', as he was sentenced to death for his beliefs and actions by the high Islamic court of Bukhara, although, unlike the historical al-Hallaj, he had a lucky escape to his homeland, where he taught his vision of Islam in the face of the hatred of his many opponents. Although his opponents were indeed many, and although even Mardzhani's father complained that it would be better for the amir of Bukhara to have killed Kursavi, he had a few friends who also studied Sufism with Ishan Niyaz of Bukhara.

Very often the Tatar ishans received their Sufi education not only in Bukhara, but also in Kabul, where the famous teacher Faez Khan Kabuli lived and taught. Interestingly, it is in the spiritual progeny of this Afghani ishan that some Russian ishans were said to possess healing and miraculous powers. One such personage was Ishan Habibullah Oryvy (1762–1816) who had his own *khanaka* in the village of Ory. This *khanaka* was so important among the population of the Mishar Tatars that, as Marzhani says, no student of Islam had a hope of becoming a mullah among the Mishars if he had not visited the *khanaka* of Ishan Habibullah and listened to his lessons. Like many of his contemporaries, Ishan Habibullah Oryvy received his Sufi initiation both in Bukhara and Kabul.

Mardzhani's grandfather was also among the disciples of this ishan, but later he became displeased with his former teacher, and he edited and corrected his writings, saying that Ishan Habibullah, towards the later part of his life, had become too worldly and lost his former spiritual attractiveness. However, the ishan had a very devoted following among his fellow Mishar Tatars. It is said that his *murids* used to kiss the traces of his winter sledges and bullock cart. They would also engage in club-fighting with the labourers of the local wealthy factory-owners, with whom their teacher would have arguments.

Yet another Tatar ishan who received his initiation at the hands of Faez Khan Kabuli was Jafar Safari. Mardzhani tells of his super-natural healing powers, miracle-working and ability to fall into a trance. Jafar Safari, unlike his many Sufi contemporaries in Russia, was very fond of music and wandered with his musical instruments in the Kazan and Ufa districts. There exists an anecdote that once, during his *hajj* (pilgrimage to Mecca), a storm overtook the vessel in which he and his fellow pilgrims were travelling. While all the other pilgrims, in their despair, were sending supplications to God, Jafa Safari took his *tanbur*, a stringed instrument, and started singing and dancing on the deck. When others accused him of blasphemy, he only answered that prayers of repentance ought to be performed in quiet times, whereas in the time of troubles it was necessary to lift other people's spirits. Mardzhani claims that his healing powers indeed helped the sick. He died in 1831.

As well as the Bukhara and Kabul spiritual line, the history of Sufism in European Russia could not be complete without a peculiar Daghestani line of Naqshbandiyya sheikhs who came to live in the Orenburg and Middle Volga areas. Such a Sufi sheikh was Muhammad bin Gali Daghestani, a former *kazi* (Arab. *qadi*, Islamic judge) from Daghestan who emigrated to Russia where he died in 1795. Living in the village of Kargala, famous for its Islamic and Sufi scholars, he initiated, according to Mardzhani, Abdrahman bin Sharif Kargali, Nigmatullah Tauzyhi and the first chief mufti of

Russia, Mukhametdzhan bin Husain, who occupied his post for fifty years. Of the latter, Mardzhani has nothing good to say, but it is worth mentioning that Sufi education was present at the highest and government-approved levels of the Russian Islamic hierarchy as much as it was at the lowest.

Among the Kargala Sufis, Mardzhani tells us at some length of Yahya-Ishan Barazavi who was famous for his gift of exorcising genies and seeing 'the unseen', although there were some doubts as to the truthfulness of these claims. Anyhow, his *murid*, Musa Tuntari Ishan, never doubted this ability either in his teacher or in himself. Mardzhani says that during a Nauruz (new year) festival Musa Tuntari harnessed up to fifty people in the village of Mamsa, seated the local mullah in the sledges and went along the village street to gather alms for the mullah's household. Mardzhani quotes from the beliefs of Yahya-Ishan and his friend and Murid Musa Tutari, from which it transpires that both were well versed in the writings of Abu Hamid al-Ghazzali and Ibn Arabi, apparently subscribing to the *vahdat-al-vudzhud*, or 'the Unity and Oneness of Being' vision of the latter.

Looking at the available data on the history of Volga–Urals Sufism, we inevitably see that there are at least two ways in which Sufism among the Muslims of this area developed. One of these ways was by a traditional Sufi-like structure of an ishan and a number of his *murids*, whose number varied according not only to the spiritual authority of the ishan, but also according to the strength of his tribal authority. Indeed, especially among the Bashkirs and the Mishar Tatars, who in the nineteenth century still retained very strong feelings of tribal allegiance, the followers of the ishans were much stronger than those of the Kazan Tatars. This phenomenon can be illustrated not only by the writing of Mardzhani, but also by the cases of the later Sufi sheikhs and ishans of the Volga–Urals area and Siberia, the most prominent of whom were Ishan Gabidullah Kurbangaliev and Ishan Zainullah Rasulev, who represented two different, if not antagonistic trends of Sufism in Russia. They could both boast numerous followers, but their views on Islam, especially against the background of the Jadidist movement, were all but opposite, reflecting the struggle of the literalist and reformist traditions of Islam in Russia.

We can indeed speak of the reformist tradition in Russian Islam long before the start of the Jadidist movement at the end of the nineteenth century. One of the most interesting examples of this tradition would be that of Qayyum Nasiry, a Kazan Tatar scholar, whose thirst for knowledge was apparently ignited by the beliefs of his father Gabdennasir. He, like some of his contemporaries, strongly maintained that the 'doors of *ijtihad*' were not closed and that a Muslim, let alone a Sufi, should ponder over the Islamic Revelation without any restraint put on him by the earlier traditionalist and literalist understandings of Islam. Such views became the reason why he was denied the official mullah decree by the Spiritual Board in Orenburg, although de facto he was the imam of his native village of Shirdan. His son Qayyum Nasiry, the first Kazan Tatar scholar with wide encyclopaedic interests, was driven by his thirst of knowledge out of the traditional occupation of his forefathers, but the prevalent Soviet notion that he had been disappointed in Islam or Sufism does not stand up to scrutiny, because throughout his life he was inspired by Ibn Sina and other great Sufi personalities of Islamic history. At the same time, Nasiry was highly critical of some of the ishans and 'healers and miracle-workers' of his day. Being essentially a Sufi himself, he described traditional Sufi personages as 'shy in their clothing, yet arrogant in nature'. He further said: 'This world exists upon two pillars – knowledge and practical skills. If someone denies both of these pillars and claims for himself ascetic and truthful life, he will inevitably end in ignorance, greed and grabbing other people's wealth'. Reformers like Qayyum Nasiry, therefore, never belonged to any circle or brotherhood, and their loving and reverend attitude to Sufism never equalled their bitter disagreement with the Sufi ishans of their day. This attitude further showed itself in the works and philosophy of the most famous personalities of Russian Islam, the poet Gabdullah Tukay and the scholar Musa Bigiev, in whose views traditional ishanism represented the most dogmatic and regressive trends in Russian Islam.

Shigabutdin Mardzhani, an initiated Sufi, also looked for the fulfilment of his thirst for knowledge beyond traditionalist Islam, and never had *murids* of his own, unlike his much more literalist contemporaries who saw their task as securing a large following as much for political as for 'pure' Sufi purposes. The ways of Mardzhani and Nasiry brought upon them the hatred of ishans like Bahavetdin Vaisov and others who, in the eyes of the Muslims of the day, often boasted much higher spiritual authority. However, their following, large though it was, could not match single personalities who took their inspiration from the reformist trends of Mardzhani and Nasiry.

The middle of the nineteenth century in Russian Sufism also saw a turning away from the Bukharan Sufi teachers to different ones in Turkey, Egypt and Saudi Arabia. This development was not only dictated by the politics of Russian conquests in Central Asia and the Caucasus, but also by the fact that Islam in Central Asia was becoming increasingly dogmatic and traditionalist. The thirst for knowledge, therefore, sent Tatar and Bashkir Muslims in other directions, and on the threshold of the twentieth century Russian Muslim communities were to be found as far away as Hijaz itself. These communities were established mainly to help Tatar and Bashkir students survive during their studies in Turkey and Egypt, but as dogmatic Sufism in those countries was already much less interesting for them than were the new reformist trends in Islam, no prominent Sufi personality ever emerged among the Russian Muslims due to their stay abroad in the twentieth century. And yet such personalities existed in the twentieth century, even if their teachings did not originate in Russia itself. Indeed, it would be possible to say that for any demonstrative revival of Islam at the beginning of the twentieth century one has to look to Russia and its Islamic achievements, later suppressed and all but destroyed by Soviet power.

The life and work of Ishan Zainullah Rasulev, who after his death was called 'the spiritual king of his nation', are also very educative in respect of the weakening of the Central Asian and the increase of the Turkish influence. Born in 1835, Zainullah Rasulev received his religious education and his first initiation into the fold of the Naqshbandiyya in Bashkiria. In 1870, on his way to Mecca as a pilgrim, he received his second initiation in Istanbul at the hands of Sheikh Ahmad Ziyautdin Gumushenavi, the sheikh of the Khalidiya branch of Naqshbandiyya Sufism. After weeks of spiritual conversations, this sheikh bestowed upon Zainullah Rasulev the title of the

Ishan-Khalifa, and upon his return to his village in the Urals, the new Great Sheikh very soon achieved the status of a great Sufi leader and had a large following. His success brought upon him much jealousy from his contemporaries, all the more so because he was blamed for introducing the practice of the loud *dhikr* and many other 'novelties' into the traditional Sufi practices of the Volga–Urals region. For all of this, he was first subjected to interrogation by the circle of his former teacher, Ishan Gabdelkhakim Kurbangaliev, then accused of heresy by the Spiritual Board and exiled to Vologda, where he spent several years. In 1882, after his return, he was appointed imam in the town of Troitsk in the Orenburg district, where he founded the famous 'Rasuliya' *madrasa*, many students of which became well-known figures of Tatar Muslim history.

In the reformist Jadidist movement, which was based on the yearning for wider knowledge of Islam, we can definitely see traces of Sufism taken as a creative approach to religion, and nostalgia for the properly understood Revelation. In this respect among those tens of thousands of followers of whom the biographers of Ishan Rasulev speak, there were numerous personalities who played a major role in the new Jadidist understanding of Islam, opposing its traditionalist and literalist understanding. The reformist *madrasas* like 'Rasuliya' in Troitsk represent the essence of Russian Sufism, inasmuch as we understand Sufism not as a 'parallel' Islam, but as the yearning to become a 'true' Muslim, whose faith is there to help Muslim society to fulfil its latent potential in all matters without putting a brake on the individual free and creative forces within that society. In this sense, all achievements of Russian Islam to date can be seen as the fruition of Sufi thought in the nineteenth and early twentieth centuries, and in this sense Russian Sufism exists and will exist as long as the yearning for individual understanding of the Revelation is present within the Russian *umma*.

This is, however, not true of Sufism understood as a tradition of the *murshid–murid* relationship. I do not claim that such Sufi circles do not exist in Russia today, although not much is known about them, except for the fact that they are as much an import from the outside Muslim world as any other teachings of the various contemporary movements of Islam. But it seems that the 'pure' Russian tradition of ishanism is indeed difficult to find for two main reasons.

First of all, the other, except Zainullah Rasulev's, most famous Sufi brotherhoods of pre-revolutionary Russia, namely, the Kurban-galiev and Vaisov brotherhoods, both became victims of the civil war and stopped playing any significant role in Russia itself. Ishan Gabidullah Kurbangaliev, who with his many *murids*, including his son Muhammad-Gabdulkhai, took arms against the Soviets, was shot dead in 1920 on the command of the erstwhile follower of Ishan Rasulev, the student of the 'Rasuliya' *madrasa* and the famous activist of the Bashkir state authonomy and later anti-Communist émigré Zaki Validi Tugan. The story of Muhammad-Gabdulkhai is another fantastic story of Russian Islam. He left Russia after fighting the civil war against the Soviets and became the best-known religious figure in the Far East, where he built a *madrasa* and established an Islamic printing press in Tokyo. In 1939 the Japanese authorities exiled him to Manchuria, where in 1945 he was captured by the Red Army and put in jail, although not executed, which is interesting, knowing the ways of the Stalinist authorities. It seems that his renown was so great that Stalin had plans to use him for his own purposes, which remained unknown. In 1955 Muhammad-Gabdulkhai Kurbangaliev, a Sufi ishan and the progeny of the famous Sufi family of Kurbangalievs, was freed, and until 1972 fulfilled the duties of imam in the city of Cheliabinsk, i.e. in the same district where his family of hereditary ishans came from.

Interestingly, his return was eagerly awaited in the 1920s, when the east of Bashkiria was still full of his followers, and the position of the Bashkir mufti was occupied by his erstwhile teacher and a new leader of the Bashkir *murids* of the Kurbangaliev chain, Mutygullah Gataullin, or Gatai. Until 1938, when all members of the Bashkir Spiritual Board were executed in the Stalinist anti-religious purges, the authority of Ishan Kurbangaliev was very strong, but even in the 1920s the followers of Gabdulkhai Kurbangaliev were hunted down for awaiting the return of this 'anti-Soviet counter-revolutionary'.

Still, despite all the persecution of the 1930s and 1940s, some members of the Kurbangaliev brotherhood might have survived. Moreover, several purges pertaining to 'Sufi' activities were held in the Urals in the late 1940s. In 1948–9, in the Urals, a number of ishans were arrested for 'anti-Soviet' propaganda, tried and sentenced to long terms of imprisonment. Among those convicted were

Sharifulla Tlyashev and Gubaidulla Gubaidullin, as well as Ishan Muhutdin Nasretdinov of the city of Izhevsk and their *murids*. Interestingly, these groups indeed entertained some eschatological hopes, saying that after the October Revolution of 1917 the seats of power in Russia were occupied by the followers of Dajjal (Anti-Christ). Therefore they called their followers to abstain from participating in the Soviet way of life. The ishans were especially critical of the kolkhoz structures and the national policies of the Soviet authorities, proclaiming that the end of the world, which was to come through the Third World War, was nigh.

However, the anti-Islamic policies of the Soviet government in the 1960s and 70s did not leave much room for any 'unorthodox' Sufi activities, which were viewed as suspicious, as were any unofficial activities in the Soviet Union. That said, it is possible that some sort of a Sufi revival along the Kurbangaliev lines is taking place nowadays in the eastern Bashkiria and Cheliabinsk regions, and among the Mishar Tatars, whose memory of Ishan Habibullah is being revived by the nationalist press and by their own feeling of ethnic kinship. If the historic roots of the ishanism among the Tatar and Bashkir ethnic groups were strong enough to produce a new spiritual leader, we might well witness some resurrection of a sort of Sufi brotherhood even without the efforts of the Russian *ulama*, which we mentioned at the beginning of this chapter. Yet, in the light of the above, such Sufi groups springing out of ethnic allegiance would most probably repeat the ways of authoritative and literalist ishanism of Bahavetdin Vaisov, or Gabidullah Kurbangaliev, rather than follow the much wider avenue of spiritual enlightenment opened by Kursavi, Mardzhani, Zainullah Rasulev, Galimdzhan Barudi and many of their followers 'in spirit'.

Sufism in Russia today

After an interval in the 1960s, when the idea of technical revolution manifesting itself in the achievements of Russian scientists in space exploration and nuclear physics slowly exhausted itself in the minds of the younger generation, various forms of mysticism found their way into the Soviet way of thinking. These trends were brought to the Soviet Union by the cultural waves of the hippy revolution in the

West, along with rock music and a great interest in Indian spirituality. It was then that the books by Indian gurus appeared in the Soviet Union and, simultaneously, the books of Georgii Gurdjieff (Gurdzhiev) and the Russian painter and philosopher Nikolai Rerich occupied the thoughts of the people seeking spiritual self-expression. Such people started forming separate, though not very numerous groups, which knew about each other in spite of the vastness of Russia, from the capital cities of Moscow and Saint Petersburg to the Baltic states and the Russian Far East. Interest in any kind of spiritual fulfilment became so strong that members of the younger generation, mostly students, made their way out of the cities and into the 'purity' of the forests, many of them venturing as far as the mountains and taiga of Southern Siberia and the Altai.

The teachings connected with this spiritual exodus were, if anything, rather eclectic and mostly derived from Gurdjieff's writings and the books by Elena Rerich on the mysterious Shambala, the retreat of the semi-human, semi-godly Teachers of Humanity. Along the paths of the expeditions of Nikolai Rerich in the Altai mountains there appeared several 'ashrams' for spiritual meditation. At the same time, the Altai and Southern Siberia at large was a retreat for many people seeking spiritual truth in shamanism, as professing shamans were (and are) still present among the native Altai, Tuva, Khakass, Yakut and other less numerous peoples of the Soviet Union. This author, in his time, also paid tribute to the spiritual trends of the 1970s, but his search for truth along existing lines ended with disillusionment, as was the case with many of his contemporaries. This disillusionment was similar to that in the West, but if drugs killed the hippy movement of the West, its Soviet counterpart was killed by vodka, impatience and haste in attaining 'high spiritual states' without any real discipline and knowledge. Interestingly, this spiritual movement was very much atheistic in its nature, and this atheism was only appropriate for the overall eclectics of the whole enterprise.

The Soviet Union was still a closed country, and any attempts to learn mysticism from Tibet or India were impossible for the great majority. However, very soon it was discovered that one did not need to go that far if one had Central Asia on one's own doorstep. This is when Sufism as a mystic experience was suddenly remembered.

Among the Russian intelligentsia of the 1970s there was a belief that 'every bazaar' in the Central Asian republics was full of practising Sufis, of whom all kinds of miraculous stories were told and listened to. At the same time, this new interest in Sufism had little or nothing to do with Islam, and nicely fitted into a wider interest in Zen Buddhism and Eastern martial arts. However, the idea of a 'teacher–student' relationship was very important, and it was at that time that various kinds of 'spiritual masters' appeared in the European part of the Soviet Union, coming from as far away as Central Asia and Buryatia in the Far East. One of these masters became very prominent in the circles of India-obsessed seekers of truth, but his growing authority ended with a tragic incident involving one of the most popular cinema actors of the Soviet Union and thus became known to all and sundry.

This actor was Talgat Nigmatullin, the Soviet answer to Bruce Lee, whose acting talents and prowess in martial arts brought him many admirers. It was well known that one Abai, a semi-literate Sufi personality from Central Asia, became his teacher and absolute authority in the best traditions of the *murid–murshid* relationship. This Sufi personality was a frequent guest of honour in many Moscow art circles, and many then heeded his utterances. Again, his teaching was not Islamic, but no one asked that of him, as the knowledge of and faith in Islam is no more required for Sufism in its ecumenical and 'European' understanding. The sheer barbarism of what happened next shook the entire country. In Vilnius, during a lesson in total submission to his master, Talgat Nigmatullin was beaten to death in the presence of Abai by his other followers. The actor was murdered despite his pleas for mercy. The perpetrators of this crime served their prison sentences and are now free. There is little doubt that they continue with their spiritual practices, and their former fans, far from coming to their senses, see nothing wrong with what happened some twenty years ago.

Very much in line with the trends of Euro-Islam and ecumenical Sufism in the West, the present-day situation of Sufism in Russia has two distinctive features. One views Sufism in the same way as Idries Shah and Inayat Khan, whose books are widely available in the Russian language. The idea of this type of spiritual awakening has little or nothing to do with any particular religion but is rather eclectic in its nature, freely borrowing from Zen Buddhism, Hindu-ism, the Bahai faith, the writings of Gurdjieff and E. Blavatskaya and what they see as Islam. But for the most part all these borrow-ings serve to illustrate the main idea of such people, namely the possibility of unleashing one's 'hidden spiritual powers' through meditation and certain exercises without recourse to traditional religious ways of submission to God. In this respect it is under-standable that the new groups and organisations, the Russian branch of the Nimatullahi order, also known as the Moscow Sufi Society under the leadership of Leonid Tiraspolsky being most prominent of them, call themselves not religious, but cultural groupings, especially when it comes to their arguments with the Islamic authorities. The *ulama* council of Daghestan, for instance, being highly critical of Nimatullahi activities, tried to issue a *fatwa*, i.e. a statement of what should be considered correct Islam, against the order, but stopped after realising that, legally, such *cultural* activities lie beyond its sphere of competence.

At the same time the Russian followers of the order of Nimatullahi insist on calling themselves Sufis, although they admit that their Sufism is an 'un-Islamic' one. The Nimatullahi order has an active website, through which they announce their meetings in many cities of the former Soviet Union, such as Moscow, Saint Petersburg, Novosibirsk, Minsk and others. They call their meeting places *khanakas*, where the lectures of the sheikhs are held, including those of the Supreme Sheikh of the Nimatullahi order Dr Jawad Nurbakhsh. Through the same site books are sold and distributed, including those by Dr Idries Shah, Inayat Khan and others. In the face of criticism from the Russian *ulama* and other Muslims, the followers of such groups answer that their activities are not religious in nature. However, the believing Muslims in Russia are convinced that these organisations, with their ways of 'profaning' 'true' Islamic Sufism, are, in fact, created by certain powers in the world in order to drag people away from Islam as a religion. They argue that the ecumenical eclectics of such groups only borrow the outward features of the great religions, whereas the idea of God and religious laws of spiritual discipline are not present in their thinking at all.

The second feature of present-day Russian Sufism, which is much less popular and fashionable than the first one, consists in trying to find a Sufi way in and through official Russian Islam. It must be stated, however, that the semblance of an Islamic renaissance in Russia started only in 1989, when the eleven-hundredth anniversary of the official acceptance of Islam on the banks of the river Volga was celebrated across Russia. This celebration returned the *ulama* to the Russian cultural and political scene and gave them some prestige and authority that they lacked in due measure before. Still, this authority was in deep contrast with the religious search of some groups who wanted to return to the roots of 'the true Islam', unadulterated by compromises with 'novelties' and traditions of the Soviet era. In the 1980s, such groups called themselves 'Pure Islam' (Saf Islam) and it took the Russian *ulama* some effort in the 1990s to lure them back into the fold of official Islam in Russia. Today, many of the former *enfants terribles* of 'Pure Islam' serve as mullahs and muftis all over Russia, having found their place in the Islamic establishment. The search for the correct vision of Islam continues in other quarters, and it is here where the various Islamic Sufi groups also seek their own niche. However, any development of Islamic thought and practice in 1990s Russia cannot be viewed on its own, without a much wider picture of day-to-day Russian politics, especially where the question of national self-identification and self-determination is concerned.

In those Russian republics where Islam constitutes the traditional faith, i.e. Tatarstan, Bashkortostan and the republics of the Northern Caucasus, the political struggle for greater autonomy or, as in the case of Chechnya, for complete independence from the Russian Federation, at first went hand in hand with an Islamic revival. But after political measures gave the radical nationalists only so much fulfilment of their desires, the ideas of the 'revival of traditional Islam' viewed as the main foundation of national culture and history quickly gave way to much more universal visions of Islam and an Islamic state. It was then that the theories of Mawlana Mawdudi and what became known under the rather common term of Wahhabism, understood as the radical return to the purest possible Islamic roots even at the cost of national identity, paradoxically became quite useful tools in the nationalist politics of the various Russian ethnicities.

In replacing 'traditional' Islam, which in the case of Chechnya and Daghestan was, of course, the ways of the Qadiri and Nakshbandi orders, so-called Wahhabism gave the radical forces the much needed pretext of involving in their struggle for independence all other North Caucasian ethnicities, who otherwise did not, as a rule, sympathise with the pure nationalism, forcefulness and political intolerance of the Chechen liberation movement. To a certain extent this approach proved a success, inasmuch as it sowed the seeds of insurrection under the banner of the all-Caucasian Islamic state in the social soil of Daghestan as well. The war of 1999 in Daghestan, which was started from Chechnya and eventually saw the so-called Wahhabi villages of Daghestan cleansed of radical elements by the Russian army, was only a first step in the strategic vision of the Unified Islamic Caucasus, in which there is no place for any kind of Sufi peculiarities. Today, the deeply rooted traditions of Daghestani Sufism do not allow the imported radical theories of Islam to take root, but who knows what the future holds, because the fight for an Islamic state in the Caucasus is well funded by Arab and Pakistani religious organisations and individuals.

Another example of replacing the traditional and Sufi images of Islam with the imported visions of an Islamic state in order to achieve political goals can be seen in the changes undergone by the Tatar radical nationalists. If, in the beginning, they were applauding the ideas of Jadidism and Nakshbandi Sufism, very soon they turned away from these ideas altogether and started demanding the creation of an Islamic state in Tatarstan, at the same time blaming those who 'tried to replace the Quran with such current as Jadidism, Sufism and Euro-Islam'. While losing their social ground, the Tatar radical nationalist party of Ittifak declared *jihad* ('holy war') against the Russian state. All of it being, for the most part, lip service and vain ambitions for power, it came to nothing. Yet the presence of some Tatar and Bashkir individuals in the ranks of the Taliban movement in Afghanistan shows that Islamist extremism can indeed bear bitter fruit even in such a relatively stable environment as now exists in European Russia.

The existence in Russian Islam of so many imported ideas and theories has created in people's minds a kind of chaos, which will not be easy to bring into harmony. As has already been said, the long history of Russian Sufism, on the one hand, inspires people to follow the paths of the famous Sufis and Jadids of the past. On the other hand, the lack of a harmonious and all-encompassing vision of Islam and the substitution of the religious search for God with various structural ideas like the Islamic state and political *jihad* may produce revolutionary results. Even the most conservative, dogmatic and politically doubtful personalities of the Sufi past in Tatarstan, Gainan Vaisov and the notorious Ishmi Shan Dinmuhametov, to name only two, have had their day as national heroes despite their unrelenting struggle against the Jadidist revival of Islam in Tatarstan and all over Russia at the beginning of the twentieth century. In the prevailing turmoil, where the Islamic values of the past are being questioned in the light of political ideas, Muslim intellectuals prefer to stand aside from religious arguments, whereas the common folk are being confronted by many images of Islam and on-going bickering among the Russian *ulama* themselves. It is no surprise, then, that among the imported and highly political Arab and Pakistani visions of Islam, Turkish brands of Sufism also find their way onto the scene of Russian Islam. This Turkish influence is being propagated through Turkey-sponsored colleges, schools and *madrasas*, mostly in the form of the teachings of Badiuzaman Nursi. The groups of the Qadiri order, although not very numerous, are to some extent active in Tatarstan and other places, and the Russian *ulama* also trace their ideology and funds back to Turkey. Even if these influences are not very strong, they again bear witness to the fact that the present-day state of Islam in Russia does not offer everyone fulfilment either in a religious or spiritual, or in an intellectual way.

This is not to say that there are no attempts to bring fresh thought and rationalisation into Russian Islam as it is now. In this respect, the Internet offers a useful tool in propagating thoughts and ideas. One of the main Russian Islamic websites, Islam.ru, is trying to bring about a Muslim enlightenment by publishing articles on the history of Russian Sufism as well. However, any rationalisation of Sufi beliefs and practices, so clear in the writings of Ibn Arabi and other great sheikhs of Sufism, is again tangled in traditions of a miraculous nature so dear to the people, who look to religion for miracles rather than inner peace. Along with other essays on Sufism, the site publishes many articles about events contradicting the laws of nature, events in which every faithful Muslim is supposed to believe. Maybe the authors have forgotten the lamentations of the Russian Orthodox missionaries of the nineteenth and early twentieth centuries, when they complained that education, while turning Russian Christians away from their faith, only strengthened Muslims in their own religion.

Final remarks

Historically, Islam in Russia was indeed a religion that could apparently satisfy people's minds as well as their souls through the questioning of historical dogmas in a nostalgic search for Revelation. The questioning of such dogmas, which came about in the historical genesis of Islam as we know it today, is still a taboo in Russia, as it is in the outside Islamic world. But it is said that one cannot come twice into the same river, especially since its currents were effectively cut off for almost eighty years by the Communist atheism of Soviet rule. Seemingly the high level of education of the Soviet people would have made it easier to rationalise and bring closer the revival of the Islamic faith in all the richness that it offers spiritually and morally. For that certain established dogmas, which prevent heart-felt rational understanding of the faith, should be analysed from within Islam on the basis of its highest achievements of rationality, tolerance and Sufi love for all. Today, one religious group that tries rationally to question the prevailing dogmatic beliefs is the Ahmadiyya movement, which has a foothold in several cities and republics of Russia. It is seldom depicted as a Sufi movement, despite the fact that, for instance, an article in the *Encyclopaedia of Islam* sees its founder Mirza Gulam Ahmad as an Indian Sufi. However, it is no secret that the core of Ahmadiyya religious practice is very much Sufi in nature, even if the movement itself is against what is seen as a 'profanation' of the Islamic nature of Sufism and tries to distance itself from what is called Sufism today.

5

SUFISM BRIDGING EAST AND WEST

The case of the Bektashis

Thomas McElwain

The Silesian Anabaptists, who in the sixteenth century frantically appealed to the Sultan for help in the face of the Lutheran threat, never met their Bektashi brothers attached to the Ottoman army, for it never got past Vienna and came too late. However, that event was one of many examples where the confrontation between East and West on a higher political level obscures bridges that have united a common spirituality over the centuries.

The Bektashi order of dervishes is one of the most enigmatic forms of Sufism in the world. It has been called many things: the most liberal form of Islam, a radical Christianising wing of Islam, and a cover for pantheism, shamanism, drinking bouts and orgies. The rites of the order are generally shrouded in mystery, for it is essentially a secret society, and this merely adds to the rumours. Its influence on Europe goes far beyond its attachment to the Ottoman empire, even being found in the secret recesses of freemasonry as far afield as northern Europe, America and Australia.

Origins and historical development

The order grew out of the militant mysticism of Ahmed Yassavi in Central Asia, but did not become a popular movement before entering Anatolia through the mission of its supposed founder, Hajji Bektash Wali, in the thirteenth century. It thus became in some sense the competitor of the famous whirling dervishes, founded by Jalal al-Din Rumi at about the same time. It contrasted with the stately and courtly Mevlevi order of Rumi by using the common language of the people instead of Persian, using the common folk music, lyrics and instruments, and emphasising the emancipation, education and unveiling of women, a feature which has continued to be its hallmark. It contrasted finally with the Mevlevi by hiding in its bosom a strong Shiite current in its emphasis on the Shiite Imams, and continues today to revere the twelve Imams and to include their names repeatedly in its devotions.

In the beginning, the Bektashi order was no doubt very simple in both belief and ritual. It is likely that there was little ritual beyond simple sacrifice, circle prayer with the recitation of the Quran and perhaps Bible portions, and the whirling typical of dervish ritual in Anatolia. In the beginning, there may have been only seven or eight of the twelve Imams included. In spite of its emphasis on social justice and the Shiite Imams, it must have been highly mystical from the start. The only text in existence that can possibly be attributed to Hajji Bektash himself is a minuscule treatise, the Makalaat, whose major theme is that humankind must not be expected to conform to one spiritual standard. There are people for whom rigid and formalistic practice is appropriate. There are others, of different kinds, who need more freedom in belief and practice. The saint's genius and peculiarity is his recognition that different people have different needs. This has contributed to the development of Bektashism in many directions to include almost every sort of belief and practice. It is a widespread principle of the order, however, that an initiate should participate in all of the manifestations of the mystical experience, rather than focus on merely one of them.

By the sixteenth century, Bektashism had become associated with the military. It formed the rallying point for the elite Janissaries, and with its fostering of mystical devotion must have enhanced the cruelty of action for which that body is sometimes known. Its Shiite tendencies were also a threat to the Sultan from time to time, and there were suppressions of the order even before the final suppression in the 1920s by Atatürk for political reasons. The tightly knit organisation of Sufi lodges of all types was a potential vehicle of opposition and thus a threat to the government. There are rumours, however, that Atatürk himself had Bektashi connections, and it is at least true that Bektashi sympathisers today are among the most faithful admirers of Atatürk, considering that his reforms had much in common with Bektashi social aspirations.

Although Bektashism appeared in Anatolia as a popular movement as well as through the activity of missionaries, it spread throughout the empire mainly through the military. That is why remnants of the order are to be found in Europe as far as the Ottoman invasion went. There are still organised lodges in Macedonia, Bulgaria and Kosovo, and perhaps even in Hungary. The Albanian development is rather special, since it was attached to the court of the king himself. With the new independence of Albania the order has reappeared strongly, especially in the southern part of the country. However, the Communist regime was fairly successful in exterminating the earlier spirituality, and it is difficult in reconstruction to get beyond mere identity and forms.

The late fifteenth and early sixteenth centuries were a time of fixing the order. Although Bektashi poetry was even earlier recognised as the heart of Turkish literature, during this time the most famous poems proliferated and finally formed the core of the liturgy. The Hurufi doctrine, emphasising the mystical meaning of numbers, was soon to become prominent and eventually caused a fascination with numerology to become the central feature of many a Bektashi's spirituality. The characteristic dress, with the twelve-fluted turban, became prominent not earlier than this period. There is no evidence that initiation as such belonged to the early practice, and the *ayni cem*, or rite of initiation, with its roots in Indo-Iranian tradition, as well as celibacy, are probably practices of innovation through the reforms of Pir Sultan at the beginning of the sixteenth century. After this golden age, Bektashism appears to have been more static and less willing to adopt new beliefs and practices. Indeed, it had become so eclectic by this time that different strands of Bektashis have had trouble recognising each other as bearers of the same tradition.

Although the Bektashi order of dervishes is still officially illegal in Turkey, the cultural elements of the practice are maintained not only in the wonderful museum in Haci Bektash Köyü near Nevsehir in Anatolia, but in musical and literary societies throughout the country. Dance groups also perform the characteristic whirling in costume. Bektashi whirling differs from Mevlevi in being simpler and far easier to acquire. It is basically a counter-clockwise walk, although in different times and places some stylised gestures have been included. Men and women both perform together, and this is the aspect that has caused so many rumours of scandal throughout the centuries.

There were historically at least two systems of lodges forming what amounted at times to opposing groups, the hierarchy of one of them eventually being hereditary. Bektashism must therefore be seen as a proliferation of greatly diversified trends both in organisation and beliefs and practices. The system of lodges has been suppressed. But millions of Alevis throughout the country preserve a closely related form of spirituality to varying extents, although this does not often go beyond the performance of sacrifices in the countryside or singing Bektashi-Alevi songs to the accompaniment of the *baglama* (a lute-like folk instrument). Finally, there are here and there wandering or single dervishes throughout the country who maintain the deepest Bektashi spirituality, sometimes with the most vibrant religiosity that Islam and Sufism have produced. Once in a while one encounters such a person who even claims to follow the Qalandriyya (in modern times a tradition of highly independent ascetic dervishes whose adherence to an order is often unclear), but completely shaven people, a hallmark of this segment of Bektashi practice, seem to be a thing of the past. The name Kalender is still to be found among Turkish and other Alevis, and is even recorded among Appalachian Melungeons.

Spread to Europe and America

There are still functioning organisations in Europe. Groups exist in Albania. The lodge in Skopje under the direction of Halife Ibrahim is very popular. Turkish immigrants have brought the tradition to Germany and northern Europe, and the Bektashi-Alevi association in Mannheim publishes new and old material and provides a strong cultural programme not only for Alevi Turks but for interested Europeans. Interest in the Balkan forms of Bektashism has been sparked by the numerous and excellent publications in French and

German, but little in English. Finally, there appears to be a lingering dervish spirituality among many individuals who are descended from those who were influenced by the Ottomans from the sixteenth century onwards.

Perhaps one of the most colourful associated figures in Europe was the English silk merchant, Edward Elwall, who appears to have joined a lodge during one of his many business trips to Turkey. His religious affiliation, however, is somewhat ambiguous, since he is listed as a 'unitarian Quaker' as well as a sabbatarian Baptist. His wife retained membership in the Presbyterian church, and it is not certain to what extent Elwall's industry and eccentricity may be due to a Huguenot connection. Be that as it may, he returned to England to wear a gown and turban, and finally in the 1720s to be the last person in England to be tried for blasphemy. He had gone beyond mere eccentricity to deny the Holy Trinity in public, apparently interrupting a sermon in the Anglican church. He is better known, perhaps, for his philanthropy in providing a row of houses for the poor in Wolverhampton. The strange combination of liberality, social equality, mysticism and enjoyment at shocking the staid and traditional, has never left the order, despite the modern tendency to focus on history, culture, music and dance. That modern tendency is richly expressed in the growing number of Bektashi-Alevi organisations in Europe and America.

In America there may be an early Bektashi influence. Brent Kennedy postulates a survival of Turkish and Moorish prisoners set ashore in the early 1500s and having descendants among the Melungeons of the southern Appalachians. The Melungeons have been largely ignored in terms of folklore, although they are sometimes unwittingly included among the mountain people generally. There are tantalising clues to be found, such as the hide-and-seek rhyme 'Ollie hasten hoosen, Zaynel Aberdeen, If you find a loose un, Make em king or queen'. The rhyme obviously begins with a corruption of the names of the first four Imams.

There are Melungeons who retain some personal practices, but there is no organisational presence within living memory nor any record of it. Melungeons have been covering their tracks for several centuries, so it is unlikely that real evidence will turn up. Furthermore, Melungeon research is dogged by the fact that it is not politically expedient. If any Melungeons rally to Bektashism, it will generally be considered an attempt by a marginalised community to associate itself with exoticism. Another problem lies in the fact that such a population, if it actually existed, was separated from the centre of Bektashi development before it crystallised into its more stable form in the sixteenth century. It would thus represent neither the spring vitality of Bektashi origins nor the peak of its development.

Although there are rumours of Bektashi lodges in all the areas of Ottoman incursion into Europe, little evidence remains for many of them. The Eckerlin brothers who came from Strasbourg to Pennsylvania in the early 1700s were founding members of the Ephrata community. They were later expelled from the community for 'Ishmaelite' faith and found refuge among Melungeons and Indians in Appalachia. But there is little evidence of what their faith was, whether Islamic, Ismaili, Bektashi or merely unacceptable to the more orthodox Christianity of their former brethren.

But America is the home of one of the most important expatriate Bektashi communities. There are or have been Albanian Bektashi groups throughout the north-eastern United States, but the best known is the lodge formed by Baba Rexheb in 1953 near Detroit, Michigan. He has written *Islamic Mysticism and Bektashism*. A discourse analysis of his teaching was published by Frances Trix, *Spiritual Discourse: Learning with an Islamic Master* (1993). Despite the stature of Baba Rexheb, Bektashism has not attained the popularity of other Sufi orders in the West. This may be the result of Baba Rexheb's integrity in not compromising the spiritual tradition for other agendas.

Interest in Bektashism has increased in southern Albania since the political changes and the fall of Communism. However, the regime had effectively destroyed the tradition, so that little but the memory of the identity remains. Bektashism has been favoured, however, by being recognised by the new government as one of the four officially recognised religious communities. The Albanian Bektashis are presently the focus of intense missionary activity by evangelical Christians who care little for the former spirituality. Nevertheless, a re-establishment of Albanian Bektashism is likely to take place. Some Albanians are beginning to have an interest in this, but are greatly hampered in their spiritual activities by the very real physical and economic difficulties that exist in the area. The success of this will probably depend on the action of Albanian American Bektashis.

The same can be said to a lesser extent perhaps for Bulgaria, which is experiencing a Bektashi revival in some measure. This is well documented in the work of Irene Markoff, who as a music-ologist focuses on the forms of music. That focus is probably justified as well by the fact that post-Communist Bektashi resurgence is always a revitalisation movement emphasising such outwardly noticeable features. It remains to be seen to what extent Bulgarian Bektashis can regain their spiritual heritage, or whether the focus will continue to be on traditional music. In this there is a formal parallel, although for different reasons, with Bektashi-Aleviism among Turkish immigrants and students. This common focus is likely to result in a cross-fertilisation to produce a strong secular and culture-centred Bektashism in Europe among the ethnic groups traditionally attached to it. Thus Bektashism may become a way of affirming ethnic identity rather than a way to divine knowledge. A more detached view of Bulgarian Bektashism is found in the work of Jorgen Nielsen.

Beliefs and practices

There are indications of a resurgence of Bektashi spirituality, but these are not always attached to the resurgence of the cultural phenomena. This may produce diverging strands in the near future. Bektashi diversity, however, is nothing new. The various Bektashi groups in the past, for all the emphasis on love of all humankind – indeed, all creation – did not always appear to love each other. We can expect a proliferation of several Bektashi groups in the future in the West. At least three directions are now visible. The first is the cultural emphasis; the second is the spiritual emphasis in the Sufi tradition without attachment to Islamic law; the third is a spiritualisation of Islamic law without shedding its obligations.

It is difficult to describe either liturgy or beliefs and practices. These tend to vary not only from place to place, but from individual to individual. There are some features, however, which seem to be almost universal among Bektashis. The canon of accepted Scriptures is open and diverse, but always seems to include the four books, that is the Bible (the Torah, Psalms and Gospels) and the Quran. Strange as it may seem, the central Scriptures of what has become in Europe an obscure faith are easily obtainable in a well-stocked bookshop. It may be that Bektashism is the only spiritual tradition actually to use both the Quran and the Bible and to see some kind of consistency between the two books. Their interpretation, however, is likely to be highly mystical and individualistic, and to differ greatly from the traditional interpretations of Judaism, Christianity and Islam.

The central doctrines to be found in the earliest sources relate to the four gates, and the four types of people who experience them. The first gate is the gate of *sharia* or law, and this represents legalistic and formalistic religion. There are, according to Bektashi belief, people whose main religious need is to experience God as a Sovereign who must be obeyed. The second gate is the gate of *tariqa* or the dervish way. This is for people whose main religious need is to experience God as the Beloved. Such people emphasise love and often the ecstasy of realising the divine presence. The third gate is *ma'rifa* or awareness. This is the experience of the universe through realisations that go beyond human senses and rationality. In a word, it is to experience the universe as God would experience it. The fourth gate, *haqiqa* or the gate of reality, is to experience union with God to the extent that one loses awareness of separate existence. It is ineffable and cannot be put into words. There is an enormous literature, mainly in Albanian and Turkish, in which people from different areas define and refine these experiences, each with its own series of practices and duties. But there is no uniformity in those matters.

Whirling, singing Bektashi hymns, prayer seated in a circle, sacrifice and meditation are all ways of attaining and enhancing the experience of the higher gates. None of these are ideally an end in themselves. Except for the cultural interest so prevalent in both Turkey and the West, Bektashis would engage in them to the extent that they would find them useful for entering the Bektashi gates of experience. This has not prevented Bektashi music from becoming popular with some individuals in Europe and America whose main interest is music rather than spirituality or the search for truth. The typical Sufi experience of submission of the *murid* or follower to the *murshid* or leader is highly developed in the Bektashi hierarchy. Especially in Albania, the hierarchy has been quite fixed, with precise traditions for their appointment. Bektashism is then organised into lodges, sometimes inhabited by celibates, and forming the centre for a community of people who depend on the lodges for the normal round of ritual surrounding birth, maturity, marriage and death. Nevertheless, ideally all practice refers the dervish to the four gates.

Although there have been notable exceptions, Bektashis are known for their disregard of Islamic law. They are not likely to pray in prostration, fast or go on pilgrimage to Mecca. There is a tendency to ridicule the day of judgement, focusing rather on the life of here and now. Bektashis are especially famous for ignoring the Islamic prohibition of drinking alcohol, but part of this scandal is probably based on the poetic references to union with God as drunkenness. In my experience, most of the Bektashis I met in Turkey did use alcohol, and on one occasion I even found drunkenness a part of the ritual.

On the other hand, Bektashism has its own set of traditions, and there are rules that most Bektashis would be loath to break. Bektashis follow Islamic law in diet, differing from their Sunni neighbours in their adherence to the somewhat stricter Shiite practices. They avoid eating shellfish and the like, and even refer to the Bible in support of eating only fish which have both fins and scales. They are Torah-true also in their avoidance of hare and rabbit, which they will not even touch, and they will change direction if such an animal crosses their path. The justification of this is generally a reference to Shiite tradition or an anecdote from the martyrdom of Imam Husseyn at Kerbela. The threshold of any house is considered sacred and not to be touched. Thus in Bektashi-Alevi homes, the threshold is built high and must be stepped over. The shoes are left parallel to it. In those forms of Bektashism which maintain a high degree of ritual, the threshold is considered to represent Imam Ali as well as the Kaaba in Mecca. Before entering the lodge, the participant kneels to kiss the threshold, generally by kissing both doorposts and then kneeling with his or her hands on the threshold and kissing the backs of both hands. A final Bektashi practice is that of laying a spoon with the bowl of it down instead of up.

Like the Mevlevis, the Bektashis are known for their tolerance of Judaism and Christianity as well as Islam. More than the Mevlevis, they are considered to have taken on beliefs and practices from outside the Islamic tradition. This is especially true in relation to Christianity. The similarities, however, do not prove a real connection. The eclectic nature of Bektashism certainly must have made it easier for former Christians in Anatolia and Albania to accept Islam in the form of Bektashism. The similarity between the legends about Hajji Bektash and those of Saint Choralambos may not be fortuitous. The Bektashi babas or leaders function in many ways more like Christian priests than Islamic functionaries, but this is true throughout much of Shiism. Such leaders have also provided services functioning much like the Christian sacraments. The celibate order of Bektashi dervishes is hardly distinguishable from Christian monasticism. Finally, many researchers suggest that the Bektashis make a trinity of Muhammad, Ali and Allah. My own experience with Bektashis does not warrant the conclusion that they conceive of God as a trinity. On the other hand, I definitely found this 'trinitarian' belief among the Arabic-speaking Alawis or Nusairis of Adana, with whom Alevis and by extension Bektashis are sometimes confused.

So far as I know, no researchers have remarked on the similarities between Bektashis and Jews, although the historical contact with the Dönme or Muslim convert followers of the seventeenth-century 'false' Messiah Sabbetai Zwi is well known. Considering the various possibilities of contact with several Jewish communities of different kinds, that failure seems surprising. There are a number of features that might well have Jewish origins. The diet is more like Jewish *kashrut* than Sunni *halal*, differing only in the lack of regard to mixing milk and meat. Although there is nothing like the Sabbath observance of Judaism, certain actions are widely avoided on Saturdays, especially entertainment and commerce. Nails are pared early on Friday, full ablutions are made, and marriages and funerals avoided on that day. Although this is certainly not limited to Judaism, the star of David or Solomon's seal is a prominent decoration in Haci Bektash Köyü. It is found above all of the ancient wells in the area, and even on the big dipper in the large kettle in the kitchen, a utensil that is almost considered sacred. All in all,

Bektashism is particularly adapted to attracting people of either Christian or Jewish background.

Bektashi relations to other Muslims is another matter. Although the members of the order are welcome to follow any school of jurisprudence they wish, Bektashis have a bad reputation among Muslims for not following any of them with any degree of care. The common Hanafi school in Turkey is followed by those who do follow Islamic law, or then Shiite practice. But there is far more likely to be some hostility between Bektashis and other Muslims, mainly because of the common Bektashi failure to separate men and women, to avoid alcohol or, in the case of women, to cover their heads.

This hostility has produced a good deal of humour, however. Bektashi tales of Bektashis getting the best of Sunni Muslims in arguments abound. All of them are very clever, and some present Bektashi beliefs and practices in a hidden way. One of the most famous stories is that of a Bektashi who went to the mosque to pray. While in the line, shoulder to shoulder with the others, he was overheard reciting 'Ya Allah, give me a bottle of whiskey' instead of saying 'Lead us in the right path'. When the prayer was done, the scandalised people began to clamour for an explanation of his behaviour in spoiling the prayer. He answered: 'Every man asks God for whatever it is he does not have'.

Some might ask how to become a Bektashi. Because of the present limitations on Bektashism in Turkey, only those who are interested in viewing some remnants of the culture would be satisfied with a trip to that area. The Turkish government seems to have belatedly recognised the powerful potential of the extensive Alevi population, in many ways closely related to the Bektashi order, and their cultural features have received more attention since the early 1990s. The central lodge near Nevshehir, now a museum, still remains a place of pilgrimage, and the annual summer cultural and dance festival there has begun to attract tourists from many places.

Albanian Bektashism still tends to be rather nationalistic in character. Despite its poverty, with its new governmental support it may in time provide a community of interest to visitors. It has continued to foster the Bektashi principles of love and tolerance despite its strong nationalistic character and rigid hierarchy. The lodge in Skopje is probably the most accessible. A tourist appearing there and hoping to be initiated into the order might be disappointed. I have not visited the lodge myself, but I heard a report directly from a man who experienced it. He was a practising twelver Shiite, very strict in his practice. He reported that the people of the lodge are very strict in their adherence to Islamic law. It may be too orthodox for the tastes of many Europeans, and its members follow the Shiite rite strictly, including prayer in prostration, fasting, and all of the other Islamic laws. Second, the lodge is rife with the fakir trickery for which dervishism is so famous. My acquaintance related a strange experience. He was asked if he loved Imam Ali. He replied that he did. He was then shown a red-hot spike and told to thrust it through his hand if he loved Imam Ali. He said, 'I love Imam Ali, but I will not put the spike through my hand'. His guide then picked up the spike and seemed to put it through his hand. When he took it out, there was no burn or wound on the hand. Although most tourists would enjoy seeing this spectacle, it is doubtful that many would find it an interesting addition to their spiritual practices. A more interesting alternative might be contact with the cultural societies provided by and for Turkish immigrants. These can be found on the Internet by searching under the term Bekta, which avoids language differences and calls up sites in Turkish as well as German and English.

When I was in Turkey I met a Bektashi gentleman who claimed to be a descendant of the most famous Turkish poet, Yunus Emre. He was a wandering dervish, not initiated into any lodge. I was impressed with the depth of both his knowledge and spirituality, which showed that it is not only possible, but under some circumstances preferable, to avoid hierarchical organisation. The wandering dervish tradition is very ancient and is certainly as valid as any other, despite the fact that it is largely ignored today by scholars as well as by the popular masses. When I asked him who his *pir* or spiritual master was, he said: 'Allah is my *pir*'. When I asked him who his *musahip* or ritual partner was, he said 'Allah is my *musahip*'. When I asked him for the *silsila* or line of transmission of the tradition to him, he merely listed the twelve Imams. Yet, without institutions or fellows, I found him the most deeply spiritual man I met in all my travels among the Sufis of Turkey, Africa and the Middle East.

From this man I learned a number of meditative practices that can be used by an individual or a small group of friends. Two of these are completely silent meditations. The first is to follow the pulse, either without thinking anything or by repeating silently to oneself 'Haqq Haqq Haqq' ('Truth truth truth'). This can also be done aloud, and even in a group. It is concluded by saying Huu, drawing it out for about three seconds. Like Haqq, Huu is a Sufi name for God, possibly from the Arabic word for 'he', *huwa,* or even from the Hebrew name for God, YHWH.

The second meditation is to follow one's own breathing, either without thinking anything or by repeating silently to oneself as one expels the breath 'la ilaaha' and, as one breathes in, 'illallaah'. This Islamic confession of faith, there is no god but God, is thus made a part of one's very life and being. It can also be recited aloud, and even in a group. It is also concluded with Huu.

My instructor further initiated me into something reminiscent of Edward Elwall's disruption of the Anglican sermon. He took me to the central mosque in Konya, in front of the shrine of Jalal al-Din Rumi. As the afternoon prayer ended and people were pouring out of the mosque, he began to whirl slowly in the Mevlevi fashion, but awkwardly and tripping as though he were drunk. He drew angry and disgusted stares from the faithful.

I asked him why he did this, and in lieu of an answer he told me the following story. There was a man named Ali in a certain small and isolated village. His house was on the very edge of the village, and it was the poorest one of all. Ali was crippled and one might think would have drawn the sympathy of the people of the village. But he was a stranger who had come to the village years before, and had gained the reputation of a fool. The villagers were disgusted with him because he had the habit of placing his right hand over his heart and saying 'Assalaamu Alaykum' (peace to you), the traditional Islamic greeting, every time he met one of the dogs of the village. So when he became crippled, he was forced to eat only what his friends, the dogs, brought to him, because he was despised by all of the people. Finally, he died of hunger and neglect. But there was no one willing to bathe and bury him; in fact, no one in the village at first even noticed that he had died. The dogs of the village came and licked him, dug a hole in the floor of his hut, and buried him there.

At that time the *qutb* or divine representative on earth was unknown to the Sufis. All over the world, the Sufi masters were communicating with one another, asking who the *qutb* was. But no one knew. Then one of them had a dream that the *qutb* was a certain Ali living in a certain house at the edge of a certain small and isolated village. He went there to find him, but only found an empty hut.

In order to be a Bektashi of the wandering dervish sort, the main requisite would be to become a searcher of truth or *haqiqa*, the fourth gate, although Bektashi philosophy advocates submission to all four gates of spiritual practice. One needs no institution or initiation beyond taking Allah as one's master. The twelve holy Imams, apparently, suffice as a line of transmission. Whether in a simple individualistic form, or as part of a hierarchical community, Bektashism offers real challenges in terms of spiritual and social achievement. Perhaps this is the most famous saying of Hajji Bektash: 'Be master of your tongue, your hand, and your stomach'. That in itself offers a lifetime of practice.

6

SUFI CHARISMA
ON THE INTERNET

Garbi Schmidt

In this chapter I concentrate on a number of home pages that all represent the Naqshbandi order, particularly in the Western hemisphere. I describe the content of the home pages and I discuss what appear to be their goals and ambitions. How do the pages, for example, relate to the rest of the global Muslim community (*umma*) and the various interpretations of Islam's message that can be found within this community? One aspect that I give primary attendance to is how the charismatic role traditionally granted the Sufi sheikh is negotiated in the social spaces that the Internet creates.

If you make a search on the term 'Sufism' and its variations through an Internet search engine, you get tens of thousands of hits. The content of these pages shows an almost endless diversity. You may find sites that present the ideology of a particular order, pages that describe or sell Sufi literature, and you may find a number of pages that present themselves as 'anti-Sufi'. Since it is quite impossible to make a complete description of all Sufi material on the Internet, I have narrowed my description to sites that are written in English and are produced in the West. This approach makes sense in a medium that although claiming global potential is still primarily used and defined by users in Europe and North America. Although hundred of thousands of people in what is traditionally seen as the Muslim world are gaining access to the virtual space, their numbers are small compared to the number of users we find in the West. In the United States it is estimated that more than half the population have access to the Internet and 82 per cent of the global use of the Internet takes place in the West. Due to its historical development (the Internet was initially the product of the United States Defense Department), Internet demographics and the power structure of this medium, which is often claimed to be inherently democratic but is still controlled by certain habits of acting and behaving through words, English has become the dominant lingua franca. The use of English is the primary tool to claim the globality of the Net: if you exhibit your life and thoughts through this language, you have the potential to be understood and 'seen' by a global audience.

The 'mystical dimension' of Islam is affected – as is the case with other Islamic practices and interpretations – by the time and space in which the believers live. However, there is one factor within Sufism that is lacking or is less apparent in other forms of Islam: a strong charismatic element. The Sufi sheikh or spiritual leader personifies the teaching of *tariqa*. How this charisma is shaped and actualised is a central theme in this chapter. Can the Internet convey the effect of charisma, and if it can, how does this happen?

First, I must make clear what I mean by charisma, especially 'traditionalised charisma', which is the term I find most appropriate when dealing with Sufism and Sufi sheikhs. My use of the concept is inspired mainly by the German sociologist Max Weber. According to Weber, charisma is expressed within four areas. First, he uses the concept as a means to describe the possession or effect of forces that can affect and change the consistencies of this world and that we as humans are subdued to. Charisma is *in* but not *of* this world. It is found in what is ordinary but is in itself extraordinary. In spite of such (claimed) qualities, charisma is not something that exists independently. In order for humans to experience and eventually accept charisma it must be attached to an individual. Charisma is something personal – a crowd of humans or a car cannot have charisma. Weber even describes charisma as a *gift*: as something that is present in the character and personality of some individuals and that just needs to be awakened. Charisma is not something that can be learned, but is a personal quality that makes its owner different from everybody else. The gift (or the audience's belief that this gift exists) allows the charismatic person to claim that he or she is the medium of supernatural or special qualities or forces.

Weber claimed that charisma must be 'pure', thereby stressing that the person (the prophet) who is granted and incarnates charisma is independent of economic, social and political interests. The contrasting or even antagonistic relation to the existing economic and social order means that charisma creates a 'jump', a new beginning. Weber was convinced that charismatic authority in its pure form could only exist in its founding phase. The ideological purity and the independence of the existing social system and bureaucracy included in itself a potential for renewal and modernity. Although charisma is founded in and legitimised by thoughts that we associate with religion and tradition, and thus often associated with elements of tradition 'pointing back in time', it includes a dimension which is progressive and creative rather than maintaining and constituting.

As a creative force and basis for modernity charisma is, as argued above, channelled through an individual. Thereby Weber stresses the human potential for renewal within complexes of religion, and simultaneously the charismatic leader's dependency on the group. In order for charisma to work, it must be accepted and experienced. The charismatic leader or prophet needs an assembly where his or her message is legalised and granted authoritative status. This group's acceptance of the authority of the charismatic leader is essential, but it is, at the same time, what at length destroys the purity of the charisma in its original form. The reason is that the charisma within the group is structuralised, institutionalised and becomes an object of routine. As a result, tradition is created: an aspect subordinated to socio-economic interests and structures of power. The inescapable fate of charisma is that it becomes rigid or stagnates. It is time for yet another jump.

But is it always the case that a routinisation of charisma causes stagnation? Weber's description of authority as either rational-legal, traditional or charismatic seems to make a clear distinction between tradition and renewal. To him, charisma in its pure form contrasts with patriarchal superiority and institutional status quo. In this context I find it important to stress (as has been done by researchers of Islam and Sufis such as Pnina Werbner) that the antithetical relationship between charisma and tradition (routinisation) within Weberian terminology can be unified in the role and personality of the Sufi sheikh. The sheikh receives his legitimacy through a century-long tradition, but in order for this role to work

111

and to gain and keep authority, additional qualities are needed. To be a Sufi sheikh is not 'just' a profession, it also includes a question of personal ability to convince. Here we may thus talk about *traditionalised* or *routinised charisma*.

But is it at all possible to show the existence of charisma when a sheikh and a Sufi order try to extend their sphere of influence to a high-tech medium such as the Internet? How does charisma survive in a globalised world where religious authorities and teachings are continuously under attack? How are prominent media of modernity, such as the Internet, employed in that context? Is it possible that personal charisma, or the claim to charisma, may 'work' through an electronic medium, whether we talk about the possibility of believing in the existence of such charisma and its claim to truth, or the absolute opposite: of people and movements who aggressively try to prove the invalidity of such claims?

Hypertexts: are they valid sources?

Searches on the Internet are always made on an individual basis. They depend on individual knowledge of the medium, individual interest and the amount of time that a person has to conduct such a search. This in itself creates some interesting theoretical considerations. If one looks at Internet searches as sources for scholarly work, it is fair to ask whether or not they can be seen as representative.

If we approach the Internet as texts or 'hypertexts' (i.e. texts that are created through jumps and links between various pages and sites, and that accordingly do not have any clear-cut limitations or preconditioned progressive story), we may conclude that Internet documents (here not including emails) are *consultative*. As users of the Internet our searches on and through this medium are based on the assumption that such documents are viable sources for specific information: we expect them to give us access to news or knowledge of issues that we find useful, that we are curious about, or we find to be purely entertaining. The seriousness of the game is that Internet pages are without any possible effects, without any 'life', if they are not consulted. A person can create a home page, but if nobody reads it, it does not exist to anyone else but the person who created it. This aspect underlines the power of the reader: it is he or she who brings the page into existence outside the world and mind of its owner. The consultative element in the virtual world appears even stronger when we take into consideration that links between pages, and thus the flow in the text and the accumulation of knowledge, are chosen by the reader (even when the choice is affected by the number of links on the visited page that the reader may or may not choose from). We may jump from one page to another, compare different pages, make new searches simultaneously and thus create a text (an entity of various bits of information) that is our own, even though others have created the basis for it.

These circumstances affect the following (fixed) text. Studies in cyberspace are always, in one way or another, the results of 'jumping' investigations of certain bits of text, made within a certain timeframe and with a certain amount of available objects. The temporal dimension is crucial because many Internet documents are continuously subject to change. Internet searches made in preparation for this chapter took place between February and May 2000, and the pages described here may look quite different today. Some of them may even no longer exist. Furthermore, I only cover a handful of Internet documents out of the thousands that deal with Sufism. In many ways searches in cyberspace are comparable to the process of anthropological fieldwork. When doing fieldwork the anthropologist continuously makes choices: to talk with one person and not another, to participate in one meeting and not another. The anthropologist may fall sick in the afternoon of an important communal celebration and thus be unable to attend and make notes. Not being there or being there at a later point in time means withdrawing from the knowledge of a specific experience. The effect of such preconditions is crucial, affecting the creation of contacts within and the understanding of spaces of human interaction and knowledge, including the spaces of the Internet.

Charisma on the Internet

The Naqshbandiyya is one of the best-represented Sufi orders on the Internet. The number of English Internet documents exposing the teachings of the order is high, probably due to the influence of

Sheikh Hisham Kabbani, who is the deputy of the Grand Sheikh Muhammad Nazim al-Haqqani in the United States and his followers. Kabbani stands behind a large complex of Sufi Internet pages that all have the starting page 'Naqshbandi Net home page' as their starting point. The page presents itself not only as a web complex through which Internet users can learn about Sufism but also as a doorway to Islam as such on the Internet. The message of the Naqshbandi order is presented as representative of Islam. The starting page includes an extensive list of links to Islamic websites with diverse content. You may, for example, find commercial pages such as 'Islamic Shopping Network' where you can buy Persian daggers, sandalwood perfume, audiocassettes with interpretations of the Quran, in particular made by Sheikh Kabbani, and a number of other products. Another home page, 'al-Haq Books, Tapes and More', offers sale of books and cassettes, and the page 'World Ads' offers web hosting (i.e. help in creating and maintaining websites and web design). To prevent the following description from becoming too confusing, I have chosen to concentrate on material from three main pages within this massive web complex: the 'Haqqani Sufi Foundation' home page, the 'Naqshbandi Sufi Way' home page, and the 'al-Sunnah Foundation of America' home page. I concentrate on parts of the content of these pages, notably their description of the Sufi sheikhs and the so-called guest books. The guest books include collections of readers' correspondence with the founder(s) of the pages, potentially we may say as a means to claim a high level of quality, but also (though unintentionally) occasionally as the opposite. Questions that I will try to answer are, first, why is it necessary to have several pages in order to present one Sufi order and its message, and, second, how do the pages present and transmit the phenomenon that we may call 'traditionalised charisma'?

On the page 'Haqqani Sufi Foundation' the emphasis of personal charisma is not immediately apparent. Centred at the top of the page we see a colourful drawing with the words Allah and Haqq written in Arabic in the middle. Under this drawing the title of the page, the word Haqqani, is written in Latin letters. Apart from that, the page includes a number of small square green frames, all horisontally positioned, which include links to the page's various parts. Under these links we find twelve small flags which, if clicked with the mouse, allow you to read the page in languages other than English. Beneath the small flags, the page's row of 'awards' is situated: a number of small emblems in strong colours that can be said to express one aspect of the Internet's 'quality control'. The exhibition of such awards often appears as a means to claim authority and a high level of quality and prominence on the Net. It is not until we reach the end of the page that the charismatic element comes into view. Here, the page presents the order and person standing behind the page, i.e. the Haqqani Foundation, headed by Sheikh Hisham Kabbani. The central role of the sheikh is underlined by a picture of him in half profile, which, if one clicks on it with the mouse, moves the reader to a description of the sheikh's life and his mission in North America.

Looking at the page as a whole, as a starting page and distributor of a certain message, two elements are worth noticing. For one thing, it seems to be the intention of the page to reach a global audience. This intention is marked by the option of reading the page in more than one language. Second, it is significant that the page stands forth as a 'product', as a channel for the distribution of commercial items. That the page emphasises itself as copyrighted further gives it the air of a commercial company anxious to guard its market interests, rather than a religious institution wishing to guide people to closer contact with God. The commercial aspect of the Naqshbandi engagement on the Internet is even more obvious on another web-page, the 'Naqshbandi Sufi Way' page, within the order's web complex. The page is sponsored by companies such as American Express, Walt Disney and Baby.com, which all have their logos placed at the bottom of the page. Readers who shop through this page are ensured that 10–20 per cent of their payment is used for *sadaqa* (alms) for Islamic aid organisations.

What is most significant about the 'Naqshbandi Sufi Way' page, though, is how its graphic construction emphasises the aspect of charisma. Just under the central reference to God through the imprints of the words Allah (God) and Haqq (divine truth) we find the word *Haqqani*, one of the honorary names of the Grand Sheikh of the Naqshbandi order, Muhammad Nazim. Beneath this title we find a picture of Sheikh Kabbani. The graphic set-up of the page thus underlines a hierarchy and internal relationship of things in which

Allah is on top, and the sheikhs just underneath. As Allah is absolute truth, so the sheikhs carry this truth downwards to their followers or those who potentially wish to follow: the readers of the home page. We may also say that it is through this vertical relationship with the sheikhs as an essential link that their followers may develop 'upward' to a deeper understanding of their relation to God. The centrality of the sheikhs' personal roles is even more strongly emphasised if one clicks on the image of Sheikh Kabbani. The link leads to a presentation of his person and office, describing him as bestowed authority and permission to lead the devout through the spiritual stations to which God has destined them. That Kabbani's long period of learning at the feet of the Grand Sheikh has secured him the attributes of intellect and wisdom, which a true master of the Path must possess, is also stressed. It is not directly mentioned who has actually granted the sheikh permission to guide the devotees, but implicitly it appears that it is God Himself. As God chooses who is to walk the path of Sufism, so is it also God who has chosen the men who are to guide them. The idea of divine intent is a precondition for Kabbani's career, education and spiritual refinements, and for the people who find his personal qualities so credible that they accept and follow his authority and guidance.

An equal emphasis on charismatic qualities is found on the page that is attributed to Sheikh Nazim. The page describes the sheikh as

> an Imam *par excellence* of the people of sincerity; he carries the secret of sainthood . . . He has infused into the Community and the Planet, love of God and love of the lovers of God's, after it has been darkened with the smoke and fire of tribulation and terror, anger and grief. He is the Scholar of Saints and the Saint of Scholars. He is the Hidden Treasure of the Gnostics. He is the Qutb [pole] of the Seekers. He is the Ghawth [helper of mediation] of Humankind. He has revived the dead hearts. He is the Inheritor of the Prophetic Characteristics. He is wearing the Cloak of the Light of the Divine Presence. He is unique in the external knowledge and the internal knowledge. He is One in his time. He is the Orchid Tree planted in the earth of Divine Love.

One must ask oneself if this emphasis on divinely granted authority and the qualities attributed to the sheikh as an heir to the prophets may reach and convince an audience through the Internet. Are Internet pages merely means of communication for communities already in existence – those who have already acknowledged the charisma of the sheikh, or can Internet pages effectively be used as a means to proselytise outside the community? The answer to this seems to be positive, even though examples are scarce. One may be found in the guest book on the page 'Naqshbandi Sufi Way'. A person from South Africa wrote in February 1997:

> It is only through the grace and mercy of Allah Almighty that I consider the discovery of the Naqshabandi Order on the Internet to be nothing short of a prayer answered, and for me a minor miracle, for I have had a burning desire, and regularly asked Allah to meet a person that would be able to guide me that which is absolute truth.

The presence of the Naqshbandi order on the Internet is here described as a miracle, as an answer to the prayers of the writer. The order's Internet pages can thus be approached as more than a means to present a certain message: they are (at least to this reader) religious messages in themselves. However, the pages' power and credibility are closely tied to certain personal qualities: whether or not the seeker may entrust his search for absolute truth to the person to whom the pages are attributed. Religious message, presence on the web and the personality of the sheikh appear inseparable and, in this case, overtly convincing. The person in question describes his first meeting with the Naqshbandi order and Sheikh Kabbani as follows:

> Everything came to a standstill. The thing that literally made my jaw drop and make me sit absolutely straight up was the first picture that appeared on the monitor, of yourself. I was blown away! Here, for the first time I encountered a man that is not only a true Sheikh but wears the majestic turban and beard. This really touched me, for I have seen many a Sheikh without these two gifts, and could

never quite understand why? I immediately took a liking to you, and wanted to know more - so I printed out as much information as possible. It made riveting reading, and only fuelled further interest. I would never be able to continue my existence without my turban and beard. I understand that these are external manifestations and some say that everything lies within. This too I understand, yet my love for these two things is unquestionable even though I might not have the full understanding and reality of the significance thereof.

It is interesting to note what element makes Sheikh Kabbani convincing to the writer. For one thing he is presented as 'a true Sheikh', and, second, as being granted two paraphernalia: the turban and the beard. These two elements are described as gifts (not the results of a personal choice but granted by someone, most probably by God Himself), and the outcome of this giftedness is the credibility of the sheikh. The gift according to Weber is, as we may recall, an important requirement for charisma. What is further interesting is that the convincing gifts are elements manifesting tradition and identification. It is through the linkage of modernity (Internet) and traditionalism (turban and beard) that the sheikh's charisma is legitimised and allowed to work. It is through this linkage that the possibility for 'miracles' is created. And it is through adapting the turban and beard, and proclaiming the religious value of these two items, that the follower manifests his dedication to and trust in the sheikh.

When looking at the Naqshbandi order's starting page one may ask why it is necessary to create such a broad range of Internet pages that all, in one way or another, seem to convey the same message. Could it not be made simpler? A possible answer is that quantity here is an argument for authority. To present many pages, to be able to serve readers in several ways, religiously as well as commercially, creates more than a Sufi cyberspace; it also underlines symbolic magnitude, power and devotion, even when the price is linkage to multi-national corperations such as Walt Disney. The large quantity of home pages underlines a global ambition. This ambition is underlined by the option for reading the page in more than one language, together with the references and links to Naqshbandi centres in different countries such as England, Malaysia, Pakistan, Brazil and Sweden. No matter where in the world readers live and no matter how well they understand English, they are granted access to the same message. The presentation of the order as global stresses its interpretation of Islam as something absolute and all-inclusive. The claim to a truthful interpretation of Islam, if accepted by the reader, also influences the understanding of the sheikhs' authority and charisma as legitimate.

The sceptics of charisma – anti-Sufism on the Internet

Not everybody on the Internet is in favour of the Naqshbandi order and its sheikhs. Some of the reasons for this may be the highly extrovert activities of this order on and beyond the Net, and its theological claim to present Islam in its absolute form. Looking through the guest book of 'Naqshbandi.org' one finds the following mail, submitted in October 1999:

> Islamic sects like the Naqshbandi have made me sick. One day one of these people came to our mosque in southern LA. You people are so unpractical!! Get real, get into the open, get out of your big houses and smell the roses. The idea of Islam is not to dhikr [remembrance of Allah] in a room the whole day. While, that is important, it is also important to act and get involved. Also, there is no inter-cession in Islam. Sufis need to get into their heads that trying to reach Allah through a 'shaykh' is shirk. Inter-cession is completely forbidden in Islam. In Islam, every individual can access the CREATOR individually.

In the quote the sender focuses on issues that he sees as delusive or, to use his own phrase 'unpractical'. Sufis, according to him, isolate themselves from real life, from the smell of roses and the fresh air. They neither act nor engage themselves in anything. The writer gives two examples of what he finds to be impractical behaviour. First, he presents Sufis as living in big houses – in other words, they live

119

extravagantly and materialistically – and, second, he sees them as spending the entire day on *dhikr*, which according to the writer is contrary to the golden mean of Islam. To him the ritual includes an exaggerated focus on spirituality. The mail continues with a critique of the sheikh: to believe that a sheikh can function as a link between humans and God is *shirk* and thus strictly forbidden.

A critique of the Naqshbandi order and its leaders is illustrated by part or whole Internet pages, for example the page 'this is the Naqshbandiyya' that seeks to present Kabbani as a *munafiq* (religious hypocrite) and a 'mentally disabled drug addict'. In a similar way Kabbani's followers are described as 'a gang of drug addicts, conmen and thugs'. The page almost takes the form of a 'cult basher' site, seeking to reveal the falsity of the practice and teaching of the Naqshbandi 'cult' and the decadence and greed of its sheikhs. Another example is the page 'Salafipublications' that presents itself as a distributor of 'authentic' books on Islam and as 'representing the aqeedah (creed), manhaj (methodology) and ibaadah (worship) of the earlier generations, known as the Salaf us-Saalih' (the first generations of believers). In accordance with this conviction the distributors see it as their mission to fight Islamic groups and leaders that they see as corrupting the message of Islam. One person whom they are particularly against, judging by the number of pages written against him, is Sheikh Kabbani who, among other things, is called one of this age's lesser *Dajjals* (beasts, often with an eschatological connotation, who are against God).

The reaction against the Naqshbandi order and its sheikhs on the Internet mirrors similar tendencies in the world beyond. What is perhaps most significant about anti-Sufi reactions in cyberspace is the implicit awareness that such pages may reach a potentially large audience, both among Muslims and non-Muslims. The Internet becomes an arena for calls to collective action and correction, of calling Muslims to understand what Islam, according to the conviction of the organisations and individuals behind such pages, is really about. Written as they are in English, the pages also address a non-Muslim majority, both defending and defining Islam, and attempting to prove the appropriateness of Islam in a modern, Western world. This is the case for both anti-Sufi and pro-Sufi pages. Similarly, as Sufi pages emphasise the personal qualities of the sheikh as a means to get to the inner core of Islam, so do anti-Sufi sites attack such qualities as flawed.

On 7 January 1999 Sheikh Kabbani gave a speech at the American State Department entitled 'Islamic Extremism: A Powerful Threat to American National Security'. After this speech the negative reaction against him, not least on the Internet, accelerated. In the speech Kabbani expressed what he saw as a 'problem' of Muslim congregations in the United States: that they in his view were dominated by an extreme ideology. According to him, extremists had taken over 80 per cent of the mosques and radical Islam had thus spread to 80 per cent of the Muslim population in the country. Furthermore, it was mainly the younger generation who were influenced by the forces of extremism, which he described as 'anti-American' and 'brainwashed'. Due to the activities of Muslim organisations and clubs on campus, the entire American university system was possibly threatened by extreme interpretations of Islam. As a matter of fact, Kabbani claimed, most of the Muslim organisations in the United States were affected by extremism and ignorant of the big mistakes they made. What is of particular interest here is that Kabbani mentioned the Internet as a vehicle for the development of anti-American thoughts among Muslim Americans.

After this incident the Internet became a battlefield between those who found that Kabbani was right in his accusations and those who found that he had wrongfully harmed the Muslim community in the United States. MSANEWS (MSA = Muslim Students' Association), one of the largest distributors of news about Muslims and Islam, established an entire page with links to community reactions to Kabbani's controversial speech. No doubt the speech seriously harmed Kabbani's position within the American Muslim community, even among those who prior to the incident had approved of his activities. Moderate Islamic organisations such as the Islamic Society of North America, the Muslim Students' Association and the Ministry of Imam Warith Deen Muhammad united in a collective rebuttal of Kabbani's speech. The case continued for several months, judging by the electronic letters that appeared through various Muslim Internet lists and networks in the aftermath of the 'scandal'. For example, a number of emails on the matter were distributed through MSANEWS, a list which at that point had a dominant position in the West when it came to the distribution of Muslim news on the Internet.

Three aspects may be stressed here. For one thing we may say that Kabbani through his speech tried to emphasise what he understood as genuine Islam: an Islam opposing and incompatible with extremism. In that sense we may see his speech as an attempt to counter a public opinion that does not always favour Muslims. Further, it is obvious that Kabbani through a speech before a powerful American institution tried to obtain social and political influence, an ambition that we may recall is a part of the 'charismatic call'. That the societal response was not as immediate as Weber would have it is another issue. Third, the Internet proved itself as a means to mobilise attacks and counter-attacks, to claim and reclaim the core of an Islamic message and authority of interpretation, and to negotiate the essence of a community outside virtual spheres.

The home pages of the Naqshbandi order include similar reactions to what is interpreted as 'extremist' and 'radical' Islam. In the same way that a massive presence on the Internet can be argued as a means to state authority, and to underline a claim to exact knowledge of the message of Islam, so can the Internet be a means to present viewpoints on what Islam is not. To illustrate this we may look at two articles that appeared on the Naqshbandi site 'Islamic Supreme Council' in the first half of 2000. One article dealt with what was presented as radical Islam's fight with traditional Islam and the media's focus on militant Islamic groups, and the other article dealt with radical Islam in Central Asia and Caucasus. The two articles were, if scrutinised more closely, linked. One contained a speech that Kabbani gave at a conference arranged by the Islamic Supreme Council and the Johns Hopkins University in April 2000. The speech is long, but the content can be summarised as follows.

Kabbani takes as his premise the Quranic statement that God created humanity diverse (49: 13). Current technological and global development is extending the impact of this diversity through 'different philosophical, sociological, economical and political schools within the same religion'. Diversity is, as such, as stated in the Quran, not problematic, but the purpose of humanity is still to recognise its unity within the divine creation. If groups of humans, contrary to divine purpose, stick to their sense of particularity, it is an expression of the desire for power and arrogance, which disregards the needs and dignity of other humans. Arrogance and misrepresentations of Islam in the current world are mainly attributed to people who dare to interpret the religious message without any legitimate and accepted schooling in doing so. This leads to radicalisation and further fragmentation of the Muslim *umma*.

The essential problem, according to Kabbani, is about who defines the religious discourse and according to what assumptions. Traditional Islam understands religion as a pact between people and God on the basis of modesty and tolerance. According to this conviction, there cannot be any compulsion in religion. The principle of free will is, he stresses, not a part of radical Islam. To followers of such interpretations of Islam 'faith is not an alternative: it is made necessary through violence'. Kabbani particularly refers to Wahhabism and Salafiyya as movements that represent radical Islam. Such movements to him are characterised by extremism, conservatism and restriction. On the other hand, Kabbani does not mention any organisations by name that he finds representative of traditional Islam.

Kabbani gives several examples of what he sees as characteristic of the opposition between radical and traditional Islam. Traditional Islam is described as peace-loving, moderate, a basis for unity and based on a democratic idea of the *umma*. Radical Islam, on the other hand, is violent, dictatorial, a source of fragmentation and destructive for the *umma*. Traditional Islam is apolitical and tolerant as long as the faithful are allowed to practise their religious duties, while radical Islam is engaged in politics solely to gain power and authority. Traditional Islam is characterised by knowledge and linked to a lineage of Muslim scholars who have a profound knowledge about the religious message, while radical Islam is characterised by a lack of knowledge, dilettantism and wrongful guidance.

One may ask oneself whether Kabbani loses part of his own argument and status by stating that radical Islam 'loves authority'. Is authority not an essential part of his role as a sheikh? Are we talking about two different kinds of authority? Here, it is interesting to notice the title that Kabbani uses for himself, that is Khalifa. This title may first of all be understood as referring to his status as Sheikh

Nazim's deputy in North America but, simultaneously, which
Kabbani also does, as referring to a certain historical process: how
the Muslim community after the death of the Prophet chose a new
leader. Kabbani describes the process as democratic, since it was
based on *shura* (council). As a Sufi sheikh, Kabbani has the
authority and permission to lead his followers to the spiritual states
that God has prepared for them. He does not have his position as a
result of personal ambition, but due to the fact that his followers see
him as the most capable to lead them along the spiritual path. In this
way his authority is not of this world, it is based on tradition,
divinely instituted and exposed by his personal qualities. Radical
Islam, on the other hand, is claimed to be entirely of this world,
created by humans and without any divine interference and
permission.

That Sufi orders and Sufi sheikhs try to stay outside politics is
nothing new. Imam al-Ghazzali (d. 1111), one of the most distinguished theologians in Islam's history who got his reputation from
an integration of Islam's spiritual (Sufi) and formal (juridical) paths,
is a well-known example of this. However, Kabbani's excessive
stress on this aspect in his attack on what he calls radical Islam can,
beside the historical precedence, be seen as a reaction to the presentations of Islam and Muslims that are often found in the West.
Within the dominant Western discourse, Islam is often associated
with something radical and anti-Western. For an individual who
believes himself to represent a Muslim minority in the West, it may
be particularly important to diminish Islam's potentially political
dimension in order to increase the possibilities for peaceful co-
existence. Therefore the concept of 'tradition' and genuine Islam is
described as democratic to Westerners to whom the concept of
democracy is a social ideal. The stress on such a defensive interpretation of Islam may be more distinctly exposed (and possibly
criticised) on the Internet due to the large number of people that the
message may reach.

That Kabbani does not directly mention his order as an exponent
of what he presents as traditional Islam may surprise the reader. It is
possible that he is thereby attempting to express a certain modesty.
But it is more likely that he is trying to express traditional Islam as
an unbreakable entity, thus standing in contrast to the fragmentary

tendencies that to him characterise radical Islam – an idea we may say is clearly exposed in the content of the Naqshbandi Internet pages analysed in this chapter. One may also say that the unity aspect underlines the claim to abiding divine principles and authenticity. Given that the divine message is uniform, so must Islam as a religion, a movement and a community be too.

Afterword

A large part of this chapter has been written on the basis of the concept of charisma, especially in its traditionalised form. One may see this concept as an element in a long historical struggle about what role Islam must play in the lives of believers, how it is to be interpreted and by whom. The dichotomy between the two poles that Kabbani calls traditional and radical Islam, and what others may call Sufism and Islamism, continues both within as well as beyond the 'traditional' Muslim world, not least among Muslims in the West. That Kabbani strongly takes a position against certain movements and organisations in the United States and Europe is probably a result of the opposition that his order has encountered within these regions. According to his views on the essence of Islam, the critique raised by his opponents can only be seen as religious hypocrisy and a furthering of fragmentary tendencies within the *umma*.

The central aspect in this discussion is the concept of authority. May every believer independently interpret the sources, or is the interpretation a privilege of scholars with a certain schooling and giftedness? To the opponents of Sufism the last option is *bida*, i.e. something that stands in opposition to the Quran and the Sunna of the Prophet (the tradition about what Muhammad said and did). They claim that Sufi sheikhs take illusionary roles as mediators between humans and God. Every individual is directly responsible before God, and therefore mediators are pointless and spiritually corrupting. To Sufis such as Kabbani and his followers, on the other hand, people who represent movements such as Salafiyya, Wahhabiya and similar movements are guilty of *bida* because they reject the inner secrets of the Scripture and the unity of the Muslim *umma*. If one claims that everybody has equal rights to interpret, the faithful's goal of unity is destroyed.

As we have seen, the Internet is a medium for this type of discussion, functioning as a channel for news, discussions and attacks for the various positions: it is a means to convince and exercise power. Faster than ever before one may reach friends and foes, inside and across national borders. The Internet is, within the present world of global movement, an important means for ideological survival. That the Naqshbandi order in the United States has created a whole complex of home pages can be said to express a strategic argument for plurality and dominance. Whether this dominance also represents a large number of followers is something else, but on the Internet no membership numbers are visible. Here, it is only the number of pages and documents that can be counted.

Is Kabbani gaining any authority through the Internet? Is his charisma as a sheikh working through this medium? This chapter has illustrated that the authority and personal qualities of both Kabbani and his Grand Sheikh are central aspects of the home pages of the Naqshbani order; and it seems as if people may actually be convinced about the authenticity of the sheikh's claim to authority, judging by the statements found in the anonymous guest books of the home pages. A final example is that some within the Muslim community feel provoked by the exposure of Sheikh Kabbani, his person, activities and order on the Internet. Both camps use the Internet as a means to verbalise this dispute, thereby underlining the function of this medium as an arena for exchange of opinion and rhetoric. The charisma of Sufi sheikhs works on the Internet, but in the form of vigorous rejection as much as acceptance.

Home pages such as those created by the Naqshbandi order illustrate the extent to which traditional religious messages may be linked and furthered through modern technology, in particular information technology. The Naqshbandi order is nothing without its sheikhs, but in virtual space, which we may see as defining on its own terms, and which to a still larger extent defines the world around us, the order is nothing without its home pages. Information technology is thus both preserving and renewing, whether we deal with those who believe in a traditional religious leadership or the movements and arguments that stand forth in support or opposition to it.

7

SUFISM FOR WESTERNERS

Olav Hammer

Fritjof Schuon, the Swiss-born leader of the neo-Sufi Maryamiyya order, received divine mystical powers through a vision of the Virgin Mary. The precise contents of that vision were long shrouded in mystery. It appeared, however, that the Holy Mother had shown herself unclad to Schuon. Henceforth Schuon would also prefer to go naked as often as possible. Ritual nudity was also observed, and the leader of the order was frequently seen embracing nude women in order to impart some of his spiritual powers. To conservative suburbanites of Schuon's hometown of Bloomington, Indiana, Schuon seemed to be more like a dirty old man than a true spiritual leader. There were also charges that Schuon had performed his nude rituals with minors. He was tried in court, but was freed of all charges. Schuon's reputation may have been tarnished, but he remained a free man until his death on 5 May 1998. He had by then long lost any links with other Sufi masters. Even his former mentor, who was also a European who had adopted a highly idiosyncratic form of Sufism, had repudiated Schuon.

The fate of a man like Schuon may seem strange indeed. His interpretation of Sufism would appear unorthodox in the extreme. Yet, this bare-bones account points at some of the paradoxes and contradictions inherent in displacing an Islamic religious tradition from its context and transposing it to a quite alien environment. It is by all means common for an exotic practice to be imported to the West and adapted to suit Europeans and Americans. The military-style discipline typical of many Zen monasteries hardly suits coddled and individualistic Westerners who are mainly intent on learning a meditative technique. Nor is there any good reason to import the caste system together with the many gurus who come from India. Nevertheless, Sufism at times seems to have changed more radically than many other religious traditions. This chapter will follow just a few of the many individuals who have contributed to shaping Western forms of Sufism. Toward the end, we shall return to the question of how and why these originally staunchly Islamic movements have been so profoundly reshaped.

New religious movements

The nineteenth century saw the beginning of a new epoch in the religious history of the West. Whereas previous dissenting religious movements had typically reformulated Christian doctrines, new movements now arose that repudiated large parts of the biblical heritage. By the end of the century, Helena Blavatsky, a flamboyant Russian émigré, had managed to become the most successful of the leaders of these new religions. She combined various esoteric ideas that were widespread in the cultural undergrowth of the late nineteenth century: from astral travel and Atlantis to telepathy and reincarnation. She presented this heady mixture of occult speculation as the essence of all the great religious traditions of the world, as transmitted to her by great spiritual masters living in the Himalayas. Large numbers of seekers were attracted to her movement, hoping to chart a third course alongside a Christian orthodoxy that had lost much of its credibility and a materialistic world-view that seemed to rob life of its spiritual zest.

After a little more than a century, there are today hundreds of Westerners proclaiming themselves to be spiritual leaders and claiming to represent the best of the world's repository of spiritual wisdom: American Zen masters, British Sufi sheikhs and Swedish shamans. These are individuals whose religious identities are part and parcel of the cultural preconditions of modernity, not the least being globalisation. The world is understood to be one single place, where Islam and Buddhism, the Jewish kabbalah and Hindu yoga co-exist.

With the advent of a global religious culture, many of these traditions are profoundly altered as Western seekers appropriate them. Yoga in London is not the same as yoga in Varanasi, Sufism on the shelf of New Age bookstores in New York or Paris differs from Sufism as practised in the suburbs of Cairo or Istanbul. Specifically, the traditions that are borrowed are adjusted in order to fit a number of preconceptions characteristic of the modern West. Briefly, these received ideas are as follows. The essence of religion is an inner experience of the sacred, not a set of doctrines and rituals. This experience is at heart one and the same, regardless of which tradition one chooses to follow: Islam, Christianity and Buddhism are thus merely different manifestations of the same spiritual essence. The level of one's spiritual understanding is the product of a process of inner progress. Some individuals have progressed further along this path than others. For this reason, we can let ourselves be inspired by others, for instance by spiritual masters or by books containing spiritual insights.

The first converts

In the nineteenth century, intellectual circles already knew of Sufism as a historical phenomenon. Some medieval Sufi texts had been translated into French and English. These classic texts, however, had a very limited impact on the religious culture of the West. There were no Sufi missionaries in Europe or America, who could present Sufism as a living religious praxis. There were hardly any communities of Westerners in countries such as Iran, where Sufi orders were active. And whereas nineteenth-century American transcendentalists and theosophists read Hindu texts in order to find doctrines that could be suitably modernised and made relevant for a modern audience, there were few religious pioneers who were interested in creating a similarly Westernised form of Sufism. This process would only begin shortly after the turn of the twentieth century.

A Swedish painter, Ivan Aguéli, was one of the decisive cultural brokers to present the fundamentally Islamic practices of a Sufi order to the innovative religious circles of Europe. Aguéli was somewhat of an outsider in Swedish artistic life. He left Christian orthodoxy at an early stage and eagerly embraced the alternative religious and political ideologies of his time. He delved into the works of Emanuel Swedenborg, became an anarchist during a stay in Paris and was arrested for his political convictions. In France he also came in contact with the occult revival that was taking place during the late nineteenth century. He became a member of the Theosophical Society, and simultaneously picked up influences from Islam and Taoism. Aguéli's omnivorous religious appetite resembled that of present-day New Agers, who also pick, reinterpret and combine bits and pieces of traditions from all over the globe. However, Aguéli's sympathies for the Muslim world soon out-weighed his other interests. He visited Egypt in 1895, and returned a few years later with the intention of settling there. He soon went native, dressing in a fez and a flowing Egyptian robe. On the occasions when he visited his small hometown of Sala in Sweden, his exotic dress and manners seem to have caused quite a stir. However, Aguéli's adoption of Egyptian culture went far deeper than the espousal of a few exotic customs. He was a linguistic genius, and learned perfect Arabic. His letters and notebooks are filled with handwriting as fluent as that of a native speaker. Around the year 1900, Aguéli formally converted to Islam. Due to his formidable command of the language, he was able to proceed to study Islamic theology at the prestigious Al-Azhar University in Cairo – one of the first Westerners ever to do so.

Despite these tokens of Muslim orthodoxy, it was not mainstream Sunni Islam that interested Aguéli, who remained as much of a transcultural religious innovator as before his conversion. The Quran and the writings of Swedenborg remained side by side on his desk. In 1907, he was initiated into a branch of the Sufi Shadhiliyya order by its spiritual leader, Sheikh Abd ar-Rahman Illyash al-Kabir. Shortly thereafter, the sheikh appointed Aguéli a teacher, thus giving him the right to initiate others into the order.

After returning to Paris in 1910, Aguéli began submitting articles to a new journal called *La Gnose,* with the subtitle *Revue mensuelle consacrée à l'étude des sciences ésoteriques,* in English 'Gnosis, monthly journal dedicated to the study of the esoteric sciences'. Here, Aguéli had found a forum where he could present his view that medieval Sufism, especially as developed by the thirteenth-century mystic Ibn Arabi, was precisely such an esoteric science, i.e. a spiritual insight common to humanity that transcended the boundaries of conventional religion. Oversimplifying somewhat, one could say that Ibn Arabi had created a synthesis of Neoplatonic philosophy and Islam. God is to be found in everything, and is constantly creating the world. Ultimately, the deity is an utterly unknowable Supreme Being, but through his infinitely diverse creation he is forever revealing himself to humanity. Every individual attains his or her knowledge of the nature of God differently. Implicit in such a creed is a call for tolerance of other people's divergent ways of understanding God, and a sharp dichotomy between essence and manifestation. By basing his rather syncretistic faith on a personal interpretation of Ibn Arabi's mystical philosophy, Aguéli had become a quite unorthodox Muslim.

For some time, Aguéli remained a sole traveller in a highly unusual religious landscape. Then, however, followed an encounter that would transform him from Sufi convert and pluralistic seeker to the first link in a new religious movement. Due to his collaboration in *La Gnose*, he became acquainted with the founder of the journal, the young Frenchman René Guénon. Like Aguéli, Guénon had left Christian orthodoxy in order to experiment with a whole range of religious options. France was, at the turn of the century, the homeland of a vast number of more or less secret societies, and Guénon became a member of several such occultist and fringe masonic organisations: groups of people who believed in reincarnation, spiritualism and ritual magic. Guénon was dissatisfied with the doctrines of several such occult groups, and in 1909 founded *La Gnose* in order to spread what he felt to be the true core of the world's spiritual traditions. One of the ideas that fascinated him was the concept of a primordial religion of humankind, an *Ur*-revelation handed down through the ages. Vestiges of the primordial religion were to be found in several of the major religions. Guénon could therefore present articles on the hidden dimension of the Christian cross and on Hindu Vedanta philosophy in the same volumes of *La Gnose*, with no sense of contradiction.

It remains a fact that different religions, at least on the mundane plane of observable facts, seem to present divergent opinions on a variety of subjects. Was there any one creed that was more faithful to the primordial tradition? Whereas Aguéli saw Sufism as the foremost vehicle of divine wisdom, Guénon initially favoured Taoism,

Catholicism and certain Hindu philosophies. However, Guénon gradually approached the mystical branches of Islam. In 1912, he was formally initiated into the same order as Aguéli. Guénon, however, proved to be as unorthodox a Muslim as his mentor was. After his conversion, he remained a freemason as well as a member of the Catholic church. He continued to explore a variety of belief systems from a perspective that owed much to a distinctly Western esoteric mode of thought. The production of *La Gnose* came to a halt, but Guénon continued a highly productive career as a writer, publishing seventeen books and a stream of articles on his highly personal interpretation of the world's religions.

Guénon had thus been initiated as a Sufi, but the teachings he presented in his publications were certainly unconventional from an Islamic perspective. His religious world-view builds on a form of criticism of modern culture that is only comprehensible when one sees him as a deeply dissatisfied Westerner. Modern society, in his view, has lost its spiritual foundations. Science builds on a materialistic illusion, but most people who have understood that modernity is an evil force retreat into what Guénon scathingly called pseudoreligions. Among the worst of these are theosophy and spiritualism. The only viable option in the struggle against modernity is to return to the primordial Tradition. This Tradition is mainly to be found in the symbolism of the main religious systems. Spiritual insight affords one the key to understanding these symbols. Sufism, from this perspective, is a term designating one perspective among many from which to reach back to the primordial Tradition, rather than a set of Muslim social formations and practices.

In the late 1920s Guénon was hit by several personal tragedies. His wife and his aunt died, and a cousin with whom he had lived left him. Soon thereafter Guénon moved to Cairo, ostensibly in order to look for Sufi texts, but probably just as much in order to start a new life. He spent much of the rest of his life writing a considerable corpus of texts expounding what he believed to be the inner message not only of Sufism, but of all major religious traditions. By then, Guénon had gained an important follower, Fritjof Schuon. Schuon was born in the Swiss city of Basel in 1907. He joined the Catholic church, but whereas his brother would become a Catholic monk, Schuon soon left the church. Schuon discovered Guénon's writings in 1924 and was inspired to become yet another religious seeker with universalist aspirations, convinced that there was a basic concord between the world-views of the Upanishads, Buddhism and Islam. When Schuon left for Algeria in 1932 and was initiated into a Sufi order, it was not in order to become a Muslim, but to get to know the ancient wisdom tradition that Guénon had written about. Schuon received the power to initiate others, effectively making him more influential than his senior Guénon. The group around Schuon grew steadily throughout the 1930s.

In the realm of ideas, both men agreed that all religions are manifestations of an underlying divine metaphysics, to which they had immediate access. On the ground, however, matters were quite different. The friendship between Guénon and Schuon was stranded on religious questions, and specifically on the issue of the efficacy of the Christian sacraments. Schuon's belief that he had received a mystic experience, giving him direct insights into the primordial wisdom tradition, allowed him to construct his own religious movement, far removed from any Islamic form of Sufism. He still considered himself a Sufi and used the Muslim name Isa Nur ad-Din, but believed that he had found the true essence of Sufism hidden under the ephemeral details in which the various historical orders and traditions had clothed the tradition. Schuon's understanding of Sufism gained a considerable amount of legitimacy due to the endorsement of the Iranian-American professor of Islamic philosophy at George Washington University, Seyyed Hossein Nasr.

As a consequence of his universalistic approach, Schuon freely combined aspects of Islam, Buddhism, Hindu philosophies and several Native American traditions. Thus far his career resembled that of many other leaders of new religious movements in the West. A truly radical innovation originated in the middle of the 1960s. During a trip to Morocco, Schuon once again had a vision. The Virgin Mary showed herself to him, and physically transformed him. Henceforth, the divine force or *baraka* would emanate directly from Schuon's body and from pictures of him. Some of that force was transmitted to Badriyah, the woman he lived with. By being naked together, smaller amounts of *baraka* were deemed to reach his disciples. Texts intended for the circle of adepts explain that the mystic transformation led to Schuon gathering within himself all the properties previously found in Shiva, Krishna, Abraham, David, Christ and Muhammad. Sufi orders tend to be hierarchically constructed, with the sheikh functioning as a link between the divine and the ordinary member of the order, but Schuon's near-deification must have been unique.

Despite all the controversies surrounding traditionalist neo-Sufism, the writings of Guénon, Schuon and other authors within the same religious lineage have had, and continue to have, a considerable impact. The thought that Sufism is a manifestation of a divine tradition common to all world faiths remains attractive for many spiritual seekers.

Universal Sufism

At roughly the same time as Aguéli converted to Islam and became one of the very first Western Sufis, the first Sufi teacher from the Orient arrived in the West. However, Hazrat Inayat Khan (1882–1927) was an atypical representative of his tradition. Despite being a member of a Sufi group, the Chisti order, he did not represent the teachings and rituals of that order, but worked independently and propagated his own teachings. According to the semi-legendary accounts of Inayat Khan's life, he had already in childhood begun to manifest the signs that pointed to his future role as the founder of an ecumenical religion. Although he was raised in a Muslim family in India, he was, according to these sources, interested in Hindu mysticism. Like Jesus, he reportedly reached insight about his spiritual mission at the age of twelve. A number of miraculous events pointed to his historical role of uniting the religious heritage of East and West in one coherent message.

These events belong to the realm of hagiography rather than biography. The veracity of these accounts should be taken with a grain of salt. What this story really seems to say is that it was preordained that Inayat Khan should found a new universal creed, rather than a Muslim form of Sufism. Khan's message is indeed quite innovative. He states that the word 'religion' can be understood in two distinct senses. Each of the world's great religions, which he defines as Islam, Judaism, Christianity, Zoroastrianism, Hinduism and Buddhism, has an external form and an inner core. Religion in the external sense consists of the various doctrines, rituals and organisations. The inner message is, on the contrary, identical in all six. This core consists of the doctrine of the unity of God, and in the contention that the purpose of religion is to cultivate the inner life and the sense that God is present in everything. This implies that Khan's Sufism, according to his own definition, is an inner religion but not an outer one.

Most Muslims would find Khan's message highly controversial. It is certainly part of Islamic orthodoxy to claim that God has revealed his message through many prophets, from Adam to Muhammad. However, this revelation has become progressively clearer and Muhammad seals the line of prophets by transmitting the message without distortions. For most Muslims, Muhammad is foremost among prophets because his historical role is unique. For Inayat Khan, the role of Muhammad is to present the same message as all other founders of major religious traditions. As a symbol of this view, religious texts of all six religions are used in the rituals of the Sufi order. Similarly, the Quran is not seen as a unique divine revelation. One can perfectly well remain a Christian or a Buddhist and nonetheless join the Sufi order. His followers were also taught an eclectic mix of meditative practices, some of which were Islamic, others drawing on Hindu methods and yet others constructed from Christian elements.

Inayat Khan, who was also a musician, embarked on a combined mission and concert tour in 1910. In connection with a recital of Indian music, he met Ada Martin, who became his first disciple. Ada Martin was a fairly typical representative of the alternative religious milieu of that time. A woman of Jewish origin, she left the faith of her family in order to experiment with a variety of religious options. She came to perceive her meeting with Inayat Khan as the end of a long spiritual quest, and as a sign of her new status she adopted the name Rabia Martin. Two years later, Khan felt that she had attained a sufficient spiritual maturity to assume the role of teacher. This was a decisive break with the nearly universal praxis of Islamic Sufi movements, where only men reach the highest positions. Since then a number of women have had an elevated rank in Khan's order. Several of these women had backgrounds in the Theosophical Society, which retained its function as one of the main sites of unchurched spirituality during the first decades of the twentieth century.

Khan moved from the United States to London, and began spreading his message to a wider audience. He published *A Sufi Message of Spiritual Liberty* in 1914, began editing the journal *The Sufi* in 1915, and formally founded the Sufi order in 1916. He then embarked on extensive trips to expand the movement further, and set up branches in France, Switzerland and other countries. Inayat Khan returned to India in 1926 and died a year later. After his death, the Sufi order split. The American branch was at first led by Rabia Martin together with another disciple, Samuel Lewis. New schisms arose in 1945, when Martin formed a group called Sufism Reoriented and Lewis instituted the Sufi Islamia Ruhaniat Society. Even more eclectic than its predecessor, the Sufi Islamia Ruhaniat Society expanded Khan's original list of six traditions to encompass Taoism and a variety of more or less authentic tribal traditions. The European branch was also subject to schisms, with members of Inayat Khan's family presiding over the various groups. Leaders of all these groups have either been Westerners, or Westernised relatives of Khan's. Just like Guénon's esoteric and traditionalist form of religion, Inayat Khan's Sufism is a quintessentially Western phenomenon.

Sufism as popular fiction

Traditionalism has reached a relatively restricted number of individuals. The groups that can trace their lineage back to Inayat Khan also have a limited membership. Many more people have come into contact with Sufism through the popular books of Idries Shah (1924–96).

Shah began his career as a writer in 1956 with *Oriental Magic*, followed in 1957 by *The Secret Lore of Magic*. His most widely sold work, *The Sufis*, appeared in 1964. When Shah died in 1996, his books had sold some fifteen million copies in a dozen languages. Shah presented Sufism as a form of religious insight that was only marginally connected to the social formations and ritualised activities that scholars of Sufism generally study. In books such as *Thinkers of the East* and *The Exploits of the Incomparable Mulla*

Nasruddin, the core of Sufism is purported to be a form of spiritual wisdom subtly encoded in humorous anecdotes. One story tells of the man who has lost his key, and is looking desperately on the ground. A sympathetic neighbour asks if this is where he lost the key. 'No, I lost it at home', says the man, 'but there is more light here than in my own house'.

Given the right reading, such a story might well be understood as a parable of a spiritual quest. But who was Shah, and what credentials did he have for presenting such more or less Sufi-inspired lore to the West? Biographical notes in his books mention his ties of kinship with the prophet Muhammad as well as his affiliation with a more or less secret Sufi order in Central Asia. According to one version, he belonged to the same tradition as the controversial religious leader Georgii Gurdjieff. Other accounts claim that he was a member of a branch of the well-known Naqshbandi order. However, the identity of his sheikh and teacher remained a secret. His spiritual lineage made him a respected figure among sections of the higher echelons of British society. As the years passed by, Shah entered the exclusive ranks of those religious leaders who have become truly wealthy due to the generosity of their admirers.

Controversies arose during Shah's last years, since there seemed to be disturbing discrepancies between the autobiographical data and recoverable facts. Quite possibly there may be a link of kinship with the prophet Muhammad, but after 1300 years there must be a million people or more who are his descendants. Other elements of the autobiography would seem to be pure fiction. Idries was indeed born in India, but his father was an Afghan immigrant to England, who had married a Scottish woman. Idries Shah himself was mainly brought up in the vicinity of London. He did spend part of his youth abroad, but as far as is known not in any Central Asian monastic order but in the considerably less exotic business community of Uruguay. Pecuniary misfortunes and allegations of being involved in shady deals made him return hastily to Britain. His first book, *Oriental Magic*, appeared after he had been employed for some time at a museum on the Isle of Man that featured exhibits on magic and witchcraft. The story of his mysterious background seems to have been a fabrication, which took shape over the years.

The story of Idries Shah and his Sufi insights was deconstructed more than two decades ago by a professor of Oriental languages, Lawrence Elwell-Sutton. However, the public demand for Shah's books has continued unabated, and a number of his titles are still in print. His position in relation to Sufism as a group of historically documented movements is quite marginal. He has, however, played a significant role in representing the essence of Sufism as a non-confessional, individualistic and life-affirming distillation of spiritual wisdom.

Global Sufism

In the West, it is only over the last few years that Sufi teachers with distinct roots in an Islamic tradition have established their presence. Most of these individuals have followers among the immigrant communities from the Muslim areas of Africa, Asia and south-eastern Europe. The majority population of the countries in which these teachers reside will usually be entirely unaware of the presence of Sufi orders. Sufism for immigrant Muslims in the West and Sufism for Westerners would seem to be two quite distinct phenomena.

As one reads about the lives of the pioneers of Western neo-Sufism, one of the things that stands out is the extent to which they adapted Sufism to the needs of Westerners involved in a quest for alternative forms of religiosity. Even René Guénon, who moved to Egypt and remained there for the rest of his life, represents a radical departure from traditionally Islamic forms of Sufism. A simple comparison between Islamic Sufism and Western neo-Sufism might concentrate on five points, as set out in Table 7.1.

Why is Western neo-Sufism so different from Islamic Sufism? One important reason lies in the fact that Sufism in northern Africa and the Middle East is not only part of a Muslim religious context, but also of a local social setting. A reason for joining a Sufi order may be that one identifies oneself as a Muslim and wishes to deepen one's religious commitment. Sufism is not a practice centred on a monastic life or an existence in an ashram, as are many other Oriental traditions that have attracted Western adepts. On the contrary, after joining, one's bonds to surrounding Islamic society remain strong. Thus, there are no obvious precedents for a complete stranger with a different religious affiliation, different ethnic back-

Table 7.1 Comparison between Islamic Sufism and Western neo-Sufism

Islamic Sufism	Neo-Sufism
1 Membership in a Sufi order introduces the individual into a strong and often large social network.	Neo-Sufism is pursued as an individual quest; any collective participation is typically in small and socially marginal groups.
2 Belief and practices are framed within a culturally determined Muslim background.	Belief is universalist, can be combined with other forms of religiosity and are adapted to the perceptions Westerners have of themselves and their environment.
3 The roles of men and women are often sharply differentiated.	Western gender roles are adopted; women often reach important positions.
4 Islamic Sufism spreads through personal contacts.	Neo-Sufism is spread mainly through books.
5 Correct practice is paramount.	Experience is paramount.

ground and no family ties to join the group and begin to participate in the activities of the order. Only recently have some Muslim orders become more familiar with the Western pattern of the spiritual quest and have accepted outsiders. In time, perhaps more Sufi sheikhs will get used to having backpackers arrive on their doorsteps, hoping to be admitted to the community.

For a Western audience, the most appealing part of being a Sufi is hardly the prospect of forging social ties with other Muslims, but rather the element of spirituality in neo-Sufism. But what does the elusive term spirituality mean for a modern European or American? Behind this extremely vague term there are some culturally defined characteristics, that may be so obvious to many that they are no longer perceived as the specific products of our own culture. First, the concept of 'spirituality' is often set apart from terms such as 'religion' or 'faith'. For some, religion would appear to be the doctrines and rituals that authorities have forced upon people, whereas spirituality is the common core found under the various superficial manifestations. If one removes the idiosyncrasies that separate Hindus from Muslims and Buddhists from Christians, the same timeless essence would seem to underlie them all. The split between inner and outer religion that we saw in both Guénon's and Inayat Khan's understanding of Sufism appears to be part of the presuppositions of modern Westerners.

Without delving into the question whether there really are any universals uniting the various religious systems of the world, and what these universals might be, one can note that the idea of a perennial tradition arose because there was a need for such a concept. People in the Middle Ages lived in a world defined by their own religion. What was known of Ancient Greek philosophy was assimilated to a biblical framework. Contemporary peoples with a different faith – Jews and Muslims – were almost exclusively understood in negative terms. An important change in this attitude arose in fifteenth-century humanist circles in Italy. Scholars gradually became aware of a wider range of religious texts: kabbalistic tracts, Platonic dialogues, Neoplatonic treatises and the writings attributed to the mythic figure of Hermes Trismegistus.

The latter works especially posed a challenge to the intellectual culture of the Renaissance. The Hermetic corpus is a collection of Greek texts written in late antiquity. These writings were, however, falsely attributed to an Egyptian sage living at the time of Moses. It seemed obvious to the Renaissance thinkers that there were striking similarities between these purportedly ancient traditions and Scriptural revelation. How could an ancient philosopher have gained knowledge of religious truths at an epoch far predating the revelation afforded through the Gospels? And how could this common core of knowledge be so similar to the Platonic world-view? Some favoured the theory that there was a single core of divine knowledge, transmitted to a succession of sages from the dawn of time. According to an early version of this theory, developed by Marsilio Ficino in the mid-fifteenth century, Zarathustra, Hermes, Pythagoras, Orpheus and Plato had all received essentially the same teachings. The list was soon expanded by his follower Giovanni Pico della Mirandola to include various Islamic philosophers and Jewish kabbalists.

A century later another Renaissance humanist, Agostino Steuco, coined a term for this primeval revealed teaching. In a book published in 1540 with the title *De perenni philosophia* ('On the perennial philosophy'), he explains that most philosophies and religions – with the exception of the teachings of Martin Luther, of which he heartily disapproved – ultimately reflect a common doctrine. He defended his belief in the ultimate concord of all faiths by advancing a view of history that runs counter to the modern outlook, but which is not unlike the understanding of the past that one finds in many New Age books. In the beginning of time, wise people wandered the face of the Earth. They were blessed with a spiritual insight unmatched by any later age. This primeval wisdom has been gradually corrupted, but can be retrieved by studying ancient wisdom traditions.

Since the days of Steuco, the belief in a perennial philosophy stemming from the dawn of time has been reformulated in many ways. Steuco himself obviously had a very limited knowledge of the religions of the world. For him, the primeval philosophy was basically that of the Neoplatonic current. As the generations passed, travellers described previously unknown peoples, texts from the most diverse cultures were translated, and spokespersons for a variety of faiths presented their beliefs for a Western audience. The concept of a *philosophia perennis* was retained, but was filled with new doctrinal contents in order to accommodate new elements. The price to be paid for such a universalising approach is of course that any true divergence between traditions must be silenced, and those faiths that are too different from the imagined 'perennial philo-sophy' are excluded. All religions are said to be fundamentally identical, with the exception of those that claim to be exclusive truths. Thus only certain minority views of Islam can be included in the universalist scheme, since many mainstream forms are difficult to squeeze into the procrustean mould. This is one reason why those Sufi movements that are most unorthodox from a traditionally Islamic point of view are the ones that have met with the greatest success in the West.

In the contemporary West, 'true' religion is often understood as an inner experience, a personal spiritual quest. Thus ritual obser-vances, which are central to many religions as actually practised, are declared to have only a marginal significance. Ultimately, this understanding of the word 'religion' has its roots in the Protestant milieus of northern Europe. Especially in pietist circles, it was believed that the essence of religion was inner edification, the contact with the divine and the right for each Christian to teach and to preach. The step would seem small to declaring that each of us can receive insight into the divine by turning inwards. With the birth of Romanticism, similar ideas became increasingly familiar to educated people.

From the end of the nineteenth century, concepts such as experience, feeling and insight have received partially new meanings. The spiritual core within us has come to be understood in psychological terms. As psychology, understood as an academic discipline, freed itself from its roots in philosophy, the question of disciplinary boundary-drawing arose. A number of influential psychologists adopted an outlook close to that of the natural sciences, and attempted to apply experimental methods to the study of the human mind. Others had a more humanistic approach, and favoured studying human experience. Psychologists such as William James and Carl Gustav Jung felt that spiritual experiences were vital elements in psychological growth. Theories such as those formulated by James and Jung in turn influenced alternative spiritual movements beginning in the 1950s and 1960s. Since then, there has been a strong tendency to conflate religiosity, psychology and therapy.

Sufism is still quite a minor component in the palette of alternative religions in the West. Nevertheless, the number of books on the subject increases, and even the titles are evidence of the far-reaching changes that Sufism has undergone on its way to the New Age marketplace. Books such as *Sufism and Psychology* and *Sufism as Therapy* are only imaginable in a culture that is impregnated with the vocabulary of popular psychology. A title such as *Universal Sufism* reveals the eclectic spirit of the modern religious landscape.

If neo-Sufi movements have had such an ability to adapt to changing circumstances, one might wonder why their success has been so limited when compared with religious movements that draw on Indian, Japanese or Tibetan roots. Recent scholarship on the process of religious plurality and religious conversion shows how religions in the modern West function like products on a market. One does not change religious affiliation primarily because one is suddenly convinced of the merits of the new religion, or because of any obvious deprivation. Much of the research conducted over the last few years points at the importance of considerably more mundane factors. The success of a movement often has to do with its successful marketing strategies, and not least its ability to expand its membership by exploiting pre-existing social networks. Sufism had a slower start than many other alternative religions, and the gap to its main competitors remains large.

One of the most important single events that made Oriental religions known to a Western audience was the World Parliament of Religions, held in Chicago in 1893. Large numbers of visitors attended the various conferences, and missionaries of numerous faiths were present in order to draw attention to their traditions. Islam, however, was poorly represented, and there were no spokespersons of any Sufi groups. An alternative to the publicity that one might have gained by attending such an event would have been to begin long-term missionary work. However, some of the first attempts to import Sufism to the West were conducted by highly secretive groups. Obviously, few potential converts will be attracted if hardly anybody is aware of the existence of the religious movement, few people have ever met any of its members and their writings are not disseminated. Sufism has the added problem of being associated with Islam, a religion that many outsiders view with suspicion. Considering the fact that women are much more likely than men to become interested in a religious lifestyle, it is of course highly problematic that many Western women associate Islam with rigid patriarchal structures.

Despite the slow start, there is nevertheless a large potential market for Sufism in the West. In order to succeed in appealing to a broader audience, these movements would probably need charismatic representatives who are able to portray Sufism as an individualistic, experientially based universalist religion which specifically empowers women. Such a move would, however, appear to remove everything traditionally Sufi from neo-Sufism.

8

FROM CELTS TO KAABA

Sufism in Glastonbury

Ian K. B. Draper

Glastonbury is an unusual place. A small market town in the south-west of England, it has become a centre of alternative spiritualities in the UK. As a consequence of its historical associations and its unusual topographic features, the locality has developed as a centre for pilgrimage, in its broadest sense. People have visited this place for their own spiritual reasons, drawn, in the main, by its reputation. Some remain, some continue to come, others leave, disappointed, having found nothing. It is a place which delineates the varying and various trends in contemporary alternative spirituality: a place which provides indicators of these trends, be they Christian, Buddhist, pagan and Wiccan, New Age and, more recently, Sufi.

Location is an important aspect to Glastonbury, given the number of spiritualised sites in the vicinity of the town. Of particular significance is the Tor, an unusually steep natural hill which rises from the Somerset Levels. It is believed that this location has been the centre of sacred associations for a number of centuries. The chapel of St Michael was founded there possibly between 600 and 800 CE and the fourteenth-century tower remains on its summit. The hill has been associated with a number of myths and legends over the centuries and it has become a focus of Arthurian myths and associated with both modern and pre-Christian paganism. It has also been conferred with mysterious powers, in particular spiritual energy associated with ley lines, of which the Tor is believed to be a significant centre, lining up with a number of other 'St Michael' sites. It is believed by some that its structure is the site of a mysterious shamanistic labyrinth, amongst other interpretations, due to the terraces cut around it.

Around the Tor are other sub-sites, such as the Eggstone which is also used as a small pagan shrine, which includes rags tied to trees, a global phenomenon practised also at some Sufi sites: for example at the shrine of a Bulgarian Bektashi sheikh in the Rhondope Mountains. On the far side of the Tor, away from the town, it is possible to find a number of sites used for various rituals; it is not uncommon to come upon various ceremonies of ritual magic while visiting, especially at quiet times.

Associated with the Tor are the two springs that emerge at its base, one referred to as the Red Spring, which is at Chalice Well, and the other the White Spring, which is based at White Springs; both springs have different sources and mineral contents. The two springs also appear to have different spiritual associations, the Red Spring with a quasi-Christian tradition, the White Spring with a more pagan and shamanistic tradition.

Glastonbury is famously associated with Joseph of Arimathea. The story tells how Joseph visited the area, travelling from the Middle East through France and Cornwall, carrying the two cruets, or even the Holy Grail, from the Last Supper, reaching the Isle of Avalon, at Wearyall Hill. The story makes Glastonbury give claim to being one of the earliest Christian foundations in the world and the site of the chapel, built by Joseph, is said to be found in the grounds of the Abbey. In addition, there is a suggestion in the stories that as a child Jesus may have visited this place with his uncle, giving the location a particular spiritual significance for Christians and those who believe in the universal Christ (including, of course, Muslims). The Abbey becomes significant as a site of both historical and contemporary Christian pilgrimage, not only due to the myths and stories concerning Joseph, but because it was a politically significant monastery in the Middle Ages.

In more contemporary times, Glastonbury has become associated with various spiritual alternatives, some local, some trans-local: paganism, ceremonial magic, Buddhism, Druidism, Sai Baba, yoga, neo-shamanism and myriads of established and not so established complementary and alternative healing and medicine traditions; in addition, Glastonbury hosts a vibrant alternative culture of rave, psychotropic drugs and music.

A number of elaborate theories and speculations have centred on the sites in the locality – what Nicholas Mann calls 'geomantic mysteries': Dragon Lines, 'Arthur's Hunting Path', the Tor labyrinth, the Glastonbury Zodiac, associations with the Temple of Solomon and the geometrical significance of the St Mary Chapel. In many ways Glastonbury is the ultimate postmodern town – it appropriates and it is appropriated. It is an environment, as Marion Bowman states, which accedes that the following of one spiritual tradition need not negate the other.

Sufis in Glastonbury

As Glastonbury acts as a barometer of contemporary Western and Eastern spiritualities in the UK, and is a place which attracts many international visitors, particularly from the United States and Australia, it was inevitable that Sufism would find a place in the town. Located as it is in rural Somerset, there are few Muslims to be found in the locality and so it is not a place which has an indigenised Muslim community where Sufic expressions of spirituality and religiosity may be found as is the case of the urban centres of London, the midlands or the north of England. Consequently, any significant Muslim presence in the town arises as a consequence of a conscious and deliberate intention to engage with alternative spiritualities which can be found established there.

Perhaps the first group with explicit Sufi connections to establish themselves is the Chistiyya of Hazrat Inayat Khan, which has held meetings in Glastonbury for a number of years. Unlike many spiritual groups in the town, they have not attempted to attract members, and their meetings are advertised as for initiates only, the group being essentially quiet and unassuming. The Naqshbandiyya of Irina Tweedie also have some representation but have not attempted to advertise their presence to any extent.

Individual members of other orders or *tariqas* have also settled in the vicinity of the town, but they have not made attempts to establish any meetings or gatherings of *dhikr* ('remembrance'). Members of other Sufi groups, inevitably, have also visited the town, recognising it as a location which is something of a market stall, if not a supermarket, of alternative spiritualities. Often these engagements with Glastonbury by members of these *tariqa*s, have not been authorised by their organisational hierarchies and are simply a reflection of individual and idiosyncratic interests in the alternative spiritualities of the members concerned.

Certainly, individual members of North Africa-based *tariqas,* for example, have visited the town for spiritual reasons, to explore the alternatives on view or meet with others on the 'path'. For example, a number of Sufis, from different *tariqas,* have visited the town with the purpose of consulting with a particular shamanic individual who bears a behavioural resemblance to a *majdhub* (someone who is intoxicated in the Divine to the point of madness), although he was neither Muslim nor Sufi. In this sense, these Sufis relate to the neo-shamanic within the contemporary alternative spiritual culture rather than aligning themselves to a Christian one. This may be because they had earlier experiences with alternative and drug-assisted spiritualities in the 1960s, which initially brought them towards Sufism, predominantly through the North African experience rather than the Eastern Indo-Turkic one. The grounding of the Sufism of North Africa, being within the Maliki tradition of *fiqh* (jurisprudence), is far more existential and as a consequence there is a tendency to look to everyday experience, wherever it is located, as a significant element of the spiritual path. Additionally, there is a far greater recourse, within this tradition, to the notion of the *fitra* – the natural predisposed spirituality of humankind, the primal state. This facilitates a notion that all primal spiritualities bear the matrix of the *tawhidic* spirituality that is Islam and therefore Sufism. These individuals have also focused more on the Tor and its focus as a 'place of power' rather than other locations in the town and its vicinity, relating this sense of place to religious and spiritual pilgrimage and drawing parallels with the nature of the Islamic *hajj*; Glastonbury too, like Mecca, has its place of spiritual focus (the Tor), the hillocks (Chalice Hill and Wearyall Hill) and springs (the White and Red Springs).

The Sufi *tariqa* which has had the greatest explicit representation in Glastonbury is the Haqqaniyya of Sheikh Nazim al-Qubrusi al-Haqqani. This *tariqa* has one of the greatest representations, in terms of impact, of Sufis in Britain generally, and their more open acknowledgement of alternative spiritualities has meant that Glastonbury has become an inevitable location for establishing an active group.

The Haqqaniyya experience

Sheikh Nazim visited Glastonbury on 3 February 1999. It is not clear what prompted the visit or who arranged it, nor why the *tariqa* had taken so long to establish a group in the town, given its reputation as a place of spiritual pilgrimage. The sheikh arrived to address a capacity audience of more than 300 people at the Assembly Rooms. Many present were of the *tariqa*, but others were local, come to sample the 'Grand Master of the Naqshbandi *Tariqa*'. Sheikh Nazim started his talk: 'We are asking our meeting is a holy meeting. We are fed up from meetings that are not from the Lord of Heavens. Everywhere you will find meetings and gatherings but all of them are tasteless – no taste'. The appearance of Sheikh Nazim – elderly, in a cloak, a large turban, long beard, vulnerable but in command – was particularly pertinent given the context, and prompted twenty people to take initiation in the *tariqa*. The issue of being Muslim was not part of the discourse. Glastonbury is not the appropriate context to insist on formal orthodox religious identities, as Sheikh Nazim said in his address:

> Oh youngsters you are like my grandsons and grand-daughters. Ask to be for eternity. Make your efforts and aims for eternity, you should reach endless happiness, endless enjoyments. Don't say I am Christian, I am Protestant, I am Catholic, I am Muslim, I am Buddhist. No, it is not important. Are you asking eternity or not? Do you think that you'd like to be for eternity?

And Sheikh Nazim did not ignore the underlying discourses of Glastonbury. Addressing the issue of Jesus' supposed visit to the Isle of Avalon, he said in his talk: 'I am saying to you about Jesus Christ that he was travelling from East to West from North to South'. Privately, he told some of his disciples or *murid*s that Jesus had

148

visited Glastonbury by the power of *bismillah* (lit. 'in the name of Allah', often used on the commencement of an action), and that he had been in two places at once, in Palestine and in Glastonbury, physically rather than as a spiritual projection.

Although Sheikh Nazim engaged with the Christian aspect of Glastonbury, there were problems at the Abbey when he started to perform *salat* in the grounds and an official tried to prevent it taking place. Sheikh Nazim became angry, asking what the purpose of Muslim–Christian dialogue was if Muslims were not allowed to pray in the grounds of a Christian church. He had been given the opportunity to visit Chalice Wells and the Tor, but had chosen only to visit the Abbey. For many of those of the *tariqa* that have since moved to Glastonbury, the Abbey has become a place of particular focus.

During his visit, Sheikh Nazim affirmed Glastonbury as the 'spiritual heart of Britain', an ascription openly stated on the *tariqa*'s Glastonbury and UK website. He instructed his *murids* to move there and particularly his secretary, to establish a coffee shop to draw people. A charity shop called 'Healing Hearts' has been opened instead, which doubles as an impromptu hibiscus tea shop and casual meeting place. Not many *murids* subsequently moved and the ones that did were predominantly white converts – some in the *tariqa* speculate whether it is because they do not want to give up their city lives.

As stated above, there were already at least two other Sufi *tariqas* in Glastonbury when the Haqqaniyya established themselves in May 1999. Both are universal Sufi groups, the most active being the Chishtiyya of Inayat Khan, which meets on Thursday nights, the other being the Naqshbandiyya of Irena Tweedie. One of the Haqqaniyya, spoken to during a meeting in Glastonbury, stated that the Chishtiyya were the airforce who had spent eight years 'softening the people', and the Haqqaniyya were the ground troops, come to 'occupy' the town in the name of Sufism – an indication of the self-image that some of the Haqqaniyya have of the *tariqa* in relation to other *tariqa*s.

One of the main members and organisers of the *tariqa* in Glastonbury moved to the town in early 2000. He had previously been based in Sheffield which had a tradition of alternative healing and engaging with environmental issues. He was also the *tariqa*'s webmaster and, effectively, Glastonbury became for a while the base for the UK website. He somewhat jokingly observed that the charity shop in Glastonbury had become the headquarters of the *tariqa* in the UK; of course, many members say that the headquarters is Sheikh Nazim and wherever he is, an important emphasis given the somewhat disparate nature of the Haqqaniyya.

It is very apparent that the Haqqaniyya, from the start, wished to associate themselves with the Christian traditions of Glastonbury, engaging with the whole quasi-Christian discourse of a Celtic church which is Unitarian rather than Trinitarian, which upholds Muslim notions of unity or *tawhid*. The Tor appears to be associated much more with the pagan, with some members claiming that it is a place of many *jins* (spirits). The emphasis, in terms of the *tariqa*'s narrative in the town, is associated with the story of Joseph of Arimathea and the visit of Jesus to Glastonbury.

The *tariqa*'s associations with Islam, though, are played down in the town, with an emphasis being placed on the Sufi; hence the *dhikr* meetings are described as 'Sufi meditation'. In this, together with Sheikh Nazim's opening discourse in Glastonbury concerning not being Muslim, or Christian or Buddhist, the Haqqaniyya in the town are moving towards a universal Sufic stance, not dissimilar to the Chishtiyya of Inayat Khan with its practice of Universal Service (from the main religious traditions), and disassociating themselves from the shamanistic or pagan. The stance does not mean, however, that their Muslim identity and integrity are compromised in any significant way.

In 1999, the *tariqa* held a workshop, led by one of the German *murid*s, who had experience in running similar events, facilitating a process by which the participants would have a 'taste of death'. This involved visualisation exercises, including imagining being dead in a shroud in the grave. Held at the Chalice Well, it was well attended and successful. The focus on death suggests that it was specifically orientated to non-*murid*s or new *murid*s. Death is not a central discourse in Sufism – experienced practitioners, though aware of the existential shock of dying, do not necessarily distinguish between this world and the next.

After Sheikh Nazim's initial visit, meetings for *dhikr* were established in the town, which attract, on average, twenty people, sometimes more. They are of mixed gender, although there are also separate women's meetings. The main monthly Sunday meetings are led by either local principal members of the *tariqa* or one of the *khalifas* from London. There have also been Thursday meetings, the traditional night for Sufi *dhikr*, which attract fewer participants.

By way of illustration of the nature of the Glastonbury *dhikr*, an example is given of one of the meetings which took place on a Sunday in October 2000. This meeting was attended by about twenty people, ten men and ten women. The majority were Muslim but not necessarily members of the *tariqa*, and there were visitors who had responded to advertisements in the town inviting people to attend the 'Sufi meditation'. The event took place at the Catholic church hall. Rugs had been put on the floor and flowers were placed in front of the sheikh, who was visiting from London (the term 'sheikh' is often ascribed to senior members of the *tariqa* and does not refer here to Sheikh Nazim, but to the *khalifa* who was to lead the *dhikr*). The *dhikr* started immediately everyone was gathered, and was reduced in length compared to other locations in the UK, many present not being familiar with Arabic. Sheets with the *dhikr* in transliterated English had been passed around beforehand. The lights were low, the room lit by a single table lamp. Some people arrived late and were rebuked by the sheikh for disturbing the process of the *dhikr*; the rhythm of the *dhikr* was also poor and it was stopped while the sheikh instructed people to keep to time.

At the end, the sheikh gave a talk. The content was not dissimilar to talks given in other Haqqaniyya UK locations, adapting the teaching style of Sheikh Nazim – free-form and responding to those present rather than using a prepared text. The content of the talk engaged with the discourse of Glastonbury: 'Breathing is important in the Naqshbandi tradition. Breathe in Divine Light and breathe out to earth down the spine. Expand your boundaries to take in the Divine Light'. At the end of the talk, a flautist improvised in a Middle Eastern style and the sheikh played a small drum. Hibiscus tea, biscuits and dried fruit was passed round and the sheikh gave a *dua* (informal prayer) in English. One of the visiting members of the *tariqa* from outside Glastonbury started to give his own *dua* which focused on controversial and inappropriate Islamic political references but the sheikh quickly, but politely, intervened to prevent the indiscretion going further. A collection was made, suggested at 50 pence for each attendee, to cover the rent of the hall. The Haqqaniyya, unlike some groups in Glastonbury, are not engaged in profiteering.

The Thursday night *dhikrs* have a very different character. One held in July 2000 at St Bridget's Chapel in the 'Glastonbury Experience' was a public event which about twelve people attended, some *murid*s of Sheikh Nazim and some curious visitors who had seen the notice advertising the event in the charity shop window. When everyone had arrived, it was time for *salat ul-asr* and one of the *murids,* who had recently settled in the vicinity of the town, led this prayer. There were people present who were not Muslims and one attendee, an American who was visiting Glastonbury for a crop circle conference, joined the prayer and at the end became very anxious that he had offended people because he was not 'initiated'. He was reassured that it did not matter and that he should do what he felt comfortable with. The *dhikr* began and sheets with English transliterations were handed to those present. After the *dhikr,* hibiscus tea was served from a flask into small glasses, and a cheese sandwich, the only food that anyone had with them, was shared amongst those present, somewhat reminiscent of the 'feeding of the five thousand'. During the tea, a discussion about crop circles took place, due to the presence of the American visitor, and one of the *murids* stated that Sheikh Nazim had said that crop circles were an important message of Divine and paranormal significance, though the nature of that message was not expanded upon.

Members of the Haqqaniyya in Glastonbury, in both the two contrasting contexts of these examples of the Sunday and Thursday *dhikr*, show an aptitude to adjust to the setting and discourses of Glastonbury. Islam is subsumed into a Sufic presentation. Despite Sheikh Nazim's explicit adherence to a Sufism based on *sharia* (Islamic law), this aspect is played down in Glastonbury to engage with a particular genre of spirituality – universal and mainstream – drawing, in many ways, from the reputation of the Inayat Khan Chistiyya who had been holding meetings in the town for some years and who had particularly engaged with the spiritual healing tradition.

In November 2000, the Haqqaniyya in Glastonbury organised and hosted a major public event in the town, held at the Assembly Rooms, and since repeated at the town hall. Sheikh Nazim had given permission for a group of Dutch *murid*s to perform the whirling of Jalal al-Din Rumi of the Mawlawi *tariqa*, Sheikh Nazim having authority in that tradition through his mother. Earlier in the year, at a *mawlid* (a celebration of the Prophet's birthday) in Birmingham, this Dutch group had performed the whirling and the Glastonbury group had decided to arrange a similar event in Glastonbury to engage with the almost universal association of Sufism with the whirling dervishes, particularly in the Glastonbury context.

The event was very well organised by the main Glastonbury *murids*. The Assembly Rooms were arranged with a clear space in the middle of the hall and chairs around the edges. A mixer desk was situated towards the back of the hall, with a stage at the front for the musicians. There was a Rumi motif backdrop behind the stage and pictures of Rumi and calligraphy of *bismillah* ('In the name of God') and the *shahada* (the Muslim creed), around the walls. Towards the back, by one of the entrances to the hall, was a stall selling *tasbihs* (prayer beads used by many Muslims and especially Sufis), both wooden and plastic, Sheikh Nazim's books, *tawidh* (Quranic talismans worn for spiritual protection, often devised and written by a Sufi sheikh) in triangular leather pouches, CDs by a British Sufi band (with Haqqaniyya members), cards and joss sticks. Throughout the event, the stall appeared quiet; the *tariqa* does not generally engage with the Glastonbury commodification of spirituality although it does commodify itself to a greater degree than other Sufi *tariqa*s in the UK.

More than two hundred people attended the event, with admission being controlled by the Assembly Room staff. The event started with the *adhan* (call to prayer) followed by a recitation in English of some Rumi poetry by the main organiser. There followed a performance by the Birmingham Nasheed singers of some *qasida*s (devotional songs) and Punjabi songs, including some *qawwalis* (a form of devotional music particularly associated with the Chishti *tariqa* of northern India). During this performance, the main whirler, a Dutch Indonesian sheikh, started to whirl to the music. A talk was then given based on a text in Jill Purce's book on spirals which featured the Tor, which was related to Rumi's whirling. The musicians were seated on the stage, including a flautist, an attendee of the *dhikrs*, who also often gave performances at the Galatea Café, and the whirling performance commenced. During the performance by the Dutch group, some members of the audience were encouraged to whirl.

After the break, a German group took over the proceedings, with a group of musicians from Germany, including one of the *tariqa*'s principal *khalifas* who was playing saxophone and drum. Middle Eastern-style music was played while the whirlers danced; the music then changed to folk and blues music. At this point, the Dutch sheikh encouraged members of the audience to stand up and whirl also, implying some spiritual discernment in initiating this process. The atmosphere in the hall was reaching a climax. Suddenly the music stopped and the German sheikh started to recite the *dhikr*. It appeared that the audience then spontaneously stood up and began a form of *hadrah* (lit. 'presence' of the Divine, a practice of standing and moving to *dhikr*, often manifested spontaneously) in a Shad-hiliyya style. The German sheikh, microphone in hand, kept telling people: 'Be with yourself', 'Close your eyes', 'Don't worry', 'Don't let outside things in', 'Keep within, we are very rough' (referring, perhaps, to the Sufic notion of the *dhikr* being a process of the polishing of the 'heart' to create a mirror for the Divine). The audience were beginning to sway and were clapping in time to the *dhikr*.

The claiming of the Mawlawi *tariqa* by the Haqqanis is somewhat controversial. Some members of other Sufi groups feel that it is, to some extent, an appropriation of another tradition, even if Sheikh Nazim has authority to recruit for the *tariqa* on the basis of association with Rumi, who has become particularly popular over the past few years as an example of a universal mystic. Even some members of the Haqqaniyya have expressed serious misgivings about its use as a vehicle for public performance. In terms of establishing the Haqqaniyya in Glastonbury, it was a huge success, strengthening their profile in the town and increasing the attendance at the *dhikr*, now held in the East–West Centre.

A follow-up workshop was attended by about fifty participants. It had been described as a whirling workshop, but much of the morning was taken up with the Dutch sheikh holding an audience with the participants, and at the lunch break the group went to visit Glastonbury Abbey while the sheikh 'intuited' where the real grave of King Arthur was. Some of the participants did not return, somewhat disappointed by their experience. However, the afternoon session provided a number of opportunities for whirling. A significant number of Inayat Khan Chishtiyya were in attendance, some having travelled from Dorset especially for the workshop, while many of the other participants were visitors to Glastonbury who had signed up as part of their search for alternative spiritualities. Following these events, there appeared to be less emphasis on the whirling in the *tariqa* in Glastonbury. It was, for a time, incorporated into the format of the *dhikr*, but it often became impractical if the *dhikr* was held in a physically constrained environment; during one such *dhikr*, the room was just too small and participants were colliding with each other and the walls. It also disrupted the traditional Haqqaniyya format.

As a Sufi presence in Glastonbury, the Haqqaniyya have a significant hold. Their appearance, in *jubba* (a long tunic associated particularly with Turkish *tariqas*) and turban, their predisposition to alternative models of health and healing and concern over environmental issues, all sourced in the attitudes of Sheikh Nazim, find a comfortable place in the Glastonbury alternative scene. There have even been attempts to engage with the geomantic mysteries, and there was speculation, supported by diagrams and mathematical calculations, by one of the *murids*, presented for a time on the website, that the Lady Chapel in the Abbey had similar dimensions to the Kaaba in Mecca.

Essentially, the Haqqaniyya relate to Glastonbury not in terms of the place as such but in terms of the people that are drawn to the place. The performances at the Assembly Rooms and the holding of *dhikr* are about bringing people to the *tariqa* and engaging them in *tawhid* and transformation through a transposed spiritual methodology. However, the playing down of an Islamic agenda in favour of a Sufi agenda is very obviously appropriate for the context, but it is a controversial emphasis and one that not all the *murids* in the British context agree with.

Concluding comments

The presentation of the Haqqaniyya and, to a lesser extent, other *tariqas'* interactions with Glastonbury, can be seen as examples of how some Sufis are engaging with the contemporary British alternative spiritual context. The descriptions of these interactions of course raise many methodological issues, the obvious questions arising around how representative they are of the *tariqas* generally. Of course, they are not entirely representative, but they illustrate the adaptation and appropriation that are taking place to engage with contrasting alternative spiritual traditions and also with the individual *murids'* spiritual encounters on the Sufic path. These interactions, however, reflect essentially the experience of convert Sufis who are trying to engage with their own spiritual and religious heritage – something Georgii Gurdjieff alluded to when he asserted that if someone could not find a way in the religious tradition of their own people, then they were not ready for the Way. Each individual, according to the perspective of their particular adopted Sufi path, relates to different spiritual paradigms: Christian, New Age, shamanic. In many ways, despite there being a proselytising dimension to the activities of the Haqqaniyya in Glastonbury, those that have settled in the town or its vicinity recognise its importance as a place both spiritually and also as a haven from the impending eschatological events, as taught by Sheikh Nazim. Individuals from other *tariqas* that visit the town recognise the locality's spiritual significance too and, in many ways, Glastonbury has become a place of *ziyara* (journey with a spiritual intention and outcome). The Sufi engagement with Glastonbury, as a centre of spiritual alternatives and a place of power, suggests that, at least for some Sufis, there is evidence of the emergence of a unique European Sufism which is neither wholly traditional nor wholly universal and which, significantly, engages with Western spiritual paths and will continue to contribute to the rich diversity of British spirituality.

SELECT BIBLIOGRAPHY

Ingvar Svanberg

There is a long tradition of studying Sufism, especially within the discipline of the history of religions. Thus the literature on historical Sufism has become extensive and difficult to grasp. However, during recent decades interest in Sufism has broadened and now also includes contemporary forms. The increasing interest is found not only among anthropologists, who have encountered Sufis in their fieldwork, but also among scholars of religion and social scientists. Nowadays researchers study the different Sufi brotherhoods and their impact on various levels within societies in many parts of the world.

This brief bibliographical overview lists books and reports on Sufis in their social context, rather than studies of religious texts and theologies. Most of the titles deal with Sufi activities and groups during the last century, although a few more historical studies have been included too. First, there are some works on Sufism in general. Second, studies on Sufism in Europe and North America are listed. Third, there are works on various countries and regions. Most of the titles are in English, but a few studies in French and German have been included. The bibliography consists mainly of books, although there are also a few important articles.

Many Sufi brotherhoods present themselves on the Internet. Links to various contemporary Sufi brotherhoods can be found on the web pages www.world.std.com/~habib/sufi.html and www.arches. uga.edu/~godlas/sufism.html respectively. A comprehensive bibliography of one specific Sufi brotherhood is to be found on www. personal.umich.edu/~vika/biblio/naqshbandi_bib.html

Bibliographies

'Bibliographie: L'Islam contemporain en Europe occidentale', *Archives de Sciences Sociales des Religions*, 68:2 (1989), pp. 151–65.

Haddad, Yvonne Yazbeck, John Obert Voll and John L. Esposito, *The Contemporary Islamic Revival: A Critical Survey and Bibliography*. Bibliographies and Indexes in Religious Studies, 20. Westport: Greenwood Press, 1991.

Musulmans en Europe occidentale: Bibliographie commentée, ed. Felice Dassetto and Yves Conrad. Paris: Éditions L'Harmattan, 1996.

General

Abun–Nasr, Jamil M., *The Tijaniyya: A Sufi Order in the Modern World*. London: Oxford University Press, 1965.

Baldick, Julian, *Mystical Islam: An Introduction to Sufism*. London: Tauris, 2000.

Embodying Charisma: Modernity, Locality, and Performance of Emotion in Sufi Cults, ed. Pnina Werbner and Helene Basu. London: Routledge, 1998.

Ernst, Carl W., *Words of Ecstasy in Sufism*. Albany: State University of New York Press, 1985.

Ernst, Carl W., *The Shambhala Guide to Sufism*. Boston: Shambhala, 1997.

Ewing, Katherine Pratt, *Arguing Sainthood: Modernity, Psychoanalysis, and Islam*. Durham, NC: Duke University Press, 1997.

Frembgen, Jürgen W., *Derwische: Gelebter Sufismus*. Cologne: DuMont Buchverlag, 1986.

Frembgen, Jürgen W., *Kleidung und Ausrüstung islamischer Gottsucher: ein Beitrag zur materiellen Kultur des Derwischwesens*. Studies in Oriental Religions, 45. Wiesbaden: Harrassowitz, 1999.

Islamic Mysticism Contested: Thirteen Centuries of Controversies and Polemics, ed. F. de Jong and B. Radke. Leiden: E. J. Brill, 1999.

Islam Outside the Arab World, ed. David Westerlund and Ingvar Svanberg. London: Curzon, 1999.

Lings, Martin, *What is Sufism?* Oxford: Islamic Texts Society, 1999.

Melâmis-Bayrâmis: études sur trois mouvements mystiques musulmans, ed. Nathalie Clayer, Alexandre Popovic and Thierry Zarcone. Istanbul: Les Éditions Isis, 1998.

Naqshbandis: cheminements et situation actuelle d'un ordre mystique musulman, ed. Marc Gaborieau, Alexandre Popovic and Thierry Zarcone. Varia Turcica, 18. Istanbul: Institut Français d'Études Anatoliennes d'Istanbul, 1991.

The Naqshbandis in Western and Central Asia: Change and Continuity, ed. Elisabeth Özdalga. Swedish Research Institute in Istanbul. Transactions, 9. London: Curzon, 1999.

Nasr, Seyyed Hossein, *Sufi Essays*. London: Library of Islam, 1999.

Pourjavady, Nasrollah and Peter Lamborn Wilson, *Kings of Love: The Poetry and History of the Ni'matullahi Sufi Order*. Tehran: Imperial Iranian Academy of Philosophy, 1978.

Rawlinson, Andrew, *The Book of Enlightened Masters: Western Teachers in Eastern Traditions*. Chicago: Open Court, 1997.

Schimmel, Annemarie, *Sufismus: eine Einführung in die islamische Mystik*. Munich: Beck, 2000.

Schuon, Frithjof, *Understanding Islam*. London: World Wisdom Books, 1998.

Sedgwick, Mark J. R., 'The Heirs of Ahmad ibn Idris: The Spread and Normalization of a Sufi Order, 1799–1996'. Dissertation, Universitetet i Bergen, 1998.

Sirriyeh, Elisabeth, *Sufis and Anti-Sufis: The Defence, Rethinking and Rejection of Sufism in the Modern World*. London: Curzon, 1999.

Trimingham, J. Spencer, *The Sufi Orders in Islam*. Oxford: Clarendon Press, 1971.

Les voies d'Allah: les ordres mystiques dans l'islam des origines à aujourd'hui, ed. Alexandre Popovic and Gilles Veinstein. Paris: Fayard, 1996.

Zarcone, Thierry, 'Ahmad Yasavi: héros des nouvels républiques centralasiatiques', *Revue des Mondes Musulmans et de la Méditerranée*, 89–90 (2000), pp. 297–323.

Europe and North America

Hamès, Constant, 'L'Europe occidentale contemporaine', in *Les voies d'Allah: les ordres mystiques dans l'islam des origines à aujourd'hui*, ed. Alexandre Popovic and Gilles Veinstein. Paris: Fayard, 1996, pp. 442–7.

Hermansen, Marcia K., 'In the Garden of American Sufi-Movements: Hybrids and Perennials', in *New Trends and Developments in the World of Islam*, ed. Peter B. Clarke. London: Luzac, 1997, pp. 155–78.

Hermansen, Marcia K., 'Hybrid Identity Formations in Muslim America: The Case of American Sufi Movements', *The Muslim World*, 90 (2000), pp. 158–97.

Jironet, Karin, *The Image of Spiritual Liberty in the Sufi Movement Following Hazrat Inayat Khan*. Amsterdam: Universiteit van Amsterdam, Bureau Grafische Producties, 1998.

Keller, Carl-A., 'Le soufisme en Europe occidentale', in *Scholarly Approaches to Religion: Interreligious Perceptions and Islam*, ed. Jacques Waardenburg. Bern: Peter Lang, 1994, pp. 359–89.

Kinney, Jay, 'Sufism Comes to America', *Gnosis Magazine* (Winter 1994), pp. 18–22.

Popovic, Alexandre, *Un ordre de derviches en terre d'Europe: la Rifa'iyya*. Lausanne: L'Age d'homme, 1993.

Webb, Gisela , 'Tradition and Innovation in Contemporary American Islamic Spirituality: The Bawa Muhaiyadeen Fellowship', in *Muslim Communities in North America*, ed. Yvonne Y. Haddad and Jane I. Smith. Albany: State University of New York Press, 1994, pp. 75–108.

France

Ebin, Victoria, 'Making Room versus Creating Space: The Construction of Spacial Categories by Itinerant Mouride Traders', in *Making Muslim Space in North America and Europe*, ed. B. D. Metcalf. Berkeley: University of California Press, 1996, pp. 92–109.

The Netherlands

Landman, N., 'Sufi Orders in the Netherlands: Their Role in the Institutionalization of Islam', in *Islam in Dutch Society: Current Developments and Future Prospects*, ed. W. A. R. Shadid and P. S. van Koningsveld. Kampen: Pharos, 1992, pp. 26–39.

Great Britain

Draper, Mustafa, 'A Case Study of a Sufi Order in Britain'. MA thesis, Department of Theology, University of Birmingham, 1985.

Geaves, Ron, *The Sufis of Britain: An Exploration of Muslim Identity*. Cardiff: Cardiff Academic Press, 2000.

Werbner, Pnina, 'Stamping the Earth with the Name of Allah: Zikr and the Sacralizing of Space among British Muslims', *Cultural Anthropology*, 11:3 (1996), pp. 309–38.

Germany

Schleßmann, Ludwig, 'Sufismus in Deutschland', in *Beiträge zur Religion Umwelt–Forschung II*, ed. G. Rischede and K. Rudolph. Geographia Religionum, Bd. 7. Berlin: Dietrich Reimer Verlag, 1989, pp. 143–52.

The Balkans

Algar, Hamid, 'Some Notes on the Naqshbandi Tariqat in Bosnia', *Die Welt des Islams*, 13 (1972), pp. 168–203.

Clayer, Nathalie, *L'Albanie, pays des derviches: les ordres mystiques musulmans en Albanie à l'époque post-ottomane (1912–1967)*. Wiesbaden: Otto Harrassowitz, 1990.

Clayer, Nathalie, *Mystiques, etat et société: les Halvetis dans l'aire balkanique de la fin du XVe siècle à nos jours*. Leiden: E. J. Brill, 1994.

Popovic, Alexandre, 'The Contemporary Situation of the Muslim Mystic Orders in Yugoslavia' in *Islamic Dilemmas: Reformers, Nationalists, Industrialization*, ed. Ernest Gellner. Berlin: Mouton, 1985, pp. 240–54.

Popovic, Alexandre, 'Les Balkans post-ottomans' in *Les voies d'Allah: les ordres mystiques dans l'islam des origines à aujourd'hui*, ed. Alexandre Popovic and Gilles Veinstein. Paris: Fayard, 1996, pp. 380–8.

Russia, the Caucasus, the former Soviet Union

Bennigsen, Aleksandre and S. E. Wimbush, *Mystics and Commissars: Sufism in the Soviet Union*. London: Hurst, 1985.

Rywkin, Michael, 'The Communist Party and the Sufi Tariqat in the Checheno-Ingush Republic', *Central Asian Survey*, 10 (1991), pp. 133–45.

Zarcone, Thierry, 'Les confréries soufies en Sibérie', *Cahiers du Monde russe*, 41 (2000), pp. 279–96.

Zelkina, Anna, *In Quest for God and Freedom: The Sufi Naqshbandi Brotherhood of the North Caucasus*. London: Hurst, 1999.

Scandinavia

Svanberg, Ingvar, 'The Nordic Countries', in *Islam Outside the Arab World*, ed. David Westerlund and Ingvar Svanberg: London: Curzon, 1999, pp. 379–401.

INDEX

Abbasid establishment 2
Abd al-Qadir (sheikh) 9–10, 22, 28
Abd ar-Rahman Illyash al-Kabir (sheikh) 130
Abraham 26; 'Abrahamic tradition' 35
academic research (American) and Sufism 54–5; *see also* publications, Euro-Sufi
activism, American 39, 58–62
Adam 26
adaptability of Sufism 2, 6, 17, 62–3; between America and Europe 36–7, 127
advertising, Sufi 44–5
Africa: Sufi expansion in 3–4; *see also* North African Sufism
African Americans 5, 41, 43
Aguéli, Ivan 21, 129–31
Ahmad al-Rifai (mystic) 20
Ahmadiyya movement, in Russia 94
Ahmadiyya-Idrisiyya (order) 10
Ahmed Yassavi (poet) 68, 71, 95
Al-Azhar University, Cairo 130
Alawiyya (order) 19, 22
Albanese, Catherine 39
Albania 13, 97, 100–1, 105–6
alcohol, prohibition of 15, 103, 105

Alevis (Turkish group) 98, 104, 105
Algar, Hamid 64
Almqvist, Kurt 30–1
altruism, as Sufi ideal 2
America: Muslim population 41; Sufism in 5; *see also* religion: characteristics of, in America
Andalusia 28
Anderson, Jon 54
anti-Americanism 121; *see also* Western society
anti-Sufism 6, 119–22
Arasteh, Reza A. 48
Arberry, Arthur 25
Ashkijerrahi (order) 56
Atatürk 96–7
authority: charismatic *vs* traditional 111–12; spiritual and tribal, in Russian Sufism 82; *see also* charisma

Baba Rexheb 100
Baha al-Din (Naqshband) 18
Bakhtiar, Laleh 48, 52
Balkans 5, 6, 13
Banner, Lois 60–1
baptism, forced 75
baraka (blessing) 2, 9, 133
Barelwi organisation 17, 28
Barks, Coleman 45, 46